AF225973

Your Three *Inherent* Needs

Your Three *Inherent* Needs

Find Clinically Proven, Biblically Sound Skills to Overcome Anxiety and Depression

Kenza Haddock

RESOURCE *Publications* · Eugene, Oregon

I dedicate this book to:
my heavenly Father, my husband David, our children
Benjamin and Eliza, and the countless patients who trusted
me to walk with them through their healing journey.

Contents

Introduction

I was raised in an Islamic household. I grew up practicing the pillars of Islam in order to gain favor with God, whom I referred to as Allah. Islam is based on works; and at the age of twenty-three, through a series of unfortunate events, I found myself clinically depressed and clinically anxious, with nowhere to turn. In desperation, I cried out to God. I asked God if there was a way to have favor with him. That night, I had a dream it was the end-times, and I saw Jesus descending from a cloud wearing a white robe. That night, God answered my prayer by sending me his one and only Son. That night, God showed me that Jesus was the only way to him—not Mohammed, not works, not anything else under the sun, but the Lord Jesus Christ.

Throughout the following months, I surrendered my life to Jesus. Shortly after, God called me into the field of counseling. My passion is to teach people about the love of the Father—a love that once *truly* grasped will satisfy all the desires of their hearts. Today, I get to teach people how to be set free and maintain their freedom from anxiety, depression, tormenting thoughts, grief, and from past traumas, using Scripture-based clinical strategies!

Years into the counseling field, as I walked my patients through clinical strategies that are founded on Scripture, I watched their lives change as they were set free from anxiety, depression, grief, and more. God prompted me to share these strategies in a book, so they can reach people beyond my counseling office. When you read *Your Three Inherent Needs* and apply the strategies in this book, you can experience freedom from anxiety and depression that you'd never thought was possible!

This book is for those who are hanging on by a thread. For those who are looking for one last-ditch effort. For those who are crying out: "God where are you? God, are you real? God, can you really do something with my life?" Those who feel like they've gone too far for God to see them through eyes of mercy, never mind make something out of their lives. In this book, I'm going to walk you through the steps of reclaiming the inheritance you have in Jesus and living in the purpose that God has set for you when he said "It is finished" (see John 19:30). By now you may ask: "So, how do I get out of the mess I'm in?"—whether this mess was by your own doing or by someone else's doing. Great question!

Throughout this book, I'm going to teach you how to set your life on a foundation that will prove to be not only stable, but un-shakable. I will teach you how to meet your three inherent needs and how to maintain a sense of fulfillment that will overflow into your kids' lives and your grandkids' lives! Let's get started.

CHAPTER 1

Why Do I Have Needs?

PEOPLE FROM ALL WALKS of life have tried different outlets to gain relief from mental health disorders—to no avail. As a clinical therapist and a clinical director who has overseen clinical caseloads of thousands of patients, I've found that most of the issues discussed in a therapist's office can be condensed into one's inability to meet their inherent needs.

God created us with three inherent needs. Before the fall, these needs were met by him; and ever since the fall, people have been striving to meet their needs independently of God, without success, resulting in a rising epidemic of anxiety and depressive disorders. God promises to meet our needs; however, people fail to seek him because they don't trust that he has their best interest at heart. This book invites you to dive into the reality of your needs. You will identify how you currently attempt to meet your needs independently of God and explore your view of God. Throughout this book, I shed light on God's true nature and his relentless love for us. I also provide you with practical ways to engage in a conversation with God and develop a healthy relationship with him. The purpose of this book is for you to learn how to continuously invite God into your day-to-day life, overcome misperceived thoughts about God's nature, and seek him regularly as your ultimate Healer, in order to overcome daily mental health battles.

God created you with three inherent needs. These needs shape the lens through which you see yourself and relate to yourself and to others. Throughout this interactive book, we're going to explore the following:

- What are your needs, and where did they come from?

- How have you tried to and how do you currently strive to meet your needs?

- How can you meet your needs and feel whole?

Before we dive into your needs, we need to go back a little further to where your needs came from. It all started with creation. God created the world, and in the world, he placed a man and a woman. God called them very good. The man named Adam and the woman named Eve lived in harmony with God. Their three needs, which we will explore throughout the subsequent chapters, were met through God. One day, God told Adam and Eve that they could eat from any tree except for one. The serpent came, thwarted God's word, and deceived Eve into questioning God's character. Eve ate from the forbidden tree and gave some to her husband, which resulted in all three needs not being met, simultaneously. Now, thankfully, God didn't leave us there. Throughout Scripture, both the Old Testament and the New Testament unveil God's redemption plan. God gave Moses the law to keep people within the guardrails of his will. People kept breaking the law over and over. Then God sent prophets to warn and to encourage people. Finally, God sent Jesus to do what we could not do. Jesus lived a sinless life. He was crucified on the cross to satisfy God's wrath that was supposed to fall on you and me and all of humanity. Then, Jesus was resurrected. Jesus's resurrection was a display of God's acceptance of Jesus as the perfect sacrifice on your behalf, my behalf, and the whole world, so "that whoever believes in him shall not perish but have eternal life" (John 3:16b).

Why Do I Have Needs?

Throughout this book, we are going to explore the needs we lost in the fall of Adam and Eve. We will identify how we tend to meet our needs independently of God, and the emotional and spiritual implications of not having our needs met appropriately. Then, we will discuss God's action plan to meet our needs.

Section 1

Security

Whom have I in heaven but you?

—PS 73:25A

CHAPTER 2

My Need for Security

Our emotional well-being is dependent on our ability to feel secure within ourselves. This ability is developed at a young age and is well-established by adolescence—which means the environment you grew up in as a child sets the tone for how secure you feel.

I grew up in a family that practiced Islam, a religion that is based solely on works. By the time we moved to the States when I was twelve years old, the two unforgivable sins I grew up trying to avoid were: believing that God has a Son, and disobeying my parents, who at the time, I believed were mediators between God and me. My understanding of God was that he was a mean authoritarian being who was looking down on me with a microscope. I grew up with a strive-focused mentality, meaning I tried to get as many "good works" in before I died. I did this in hopes that I'd get to heaven and please my parents in the process, since I believed that they would also one day have a vote as to whether or not I got to heaven.

Research shows that when we feel secure, a part of our brain known as the amygdala calms down, enabling us to make objective and sound decisions. Conversely, when our sense of security is threatened, our brain sends signals to the amygdala in order to prepare for possible worst-case scenarios. These signals produce physical symptoms in our body such as racing heart, cold hands, shoulder tension, backache, fast breathing, etc. When we experience events in our lives in which our sense of security is threatened, our mind remains stuck in a hypervigilant state, which in turn causes or exasperates depression, anxiety, PTSD, and other mental health-related symptoms.

Growing up as a Muslim, my perspective of God was so far from the truth. I viewed God as a dictator who didn't care to have a relationship with me. Developing a relationship with God was a foreign concept that bordered on blasphemy. So, my view of God was reduced to certain religious rituals that I had to complete daily. If I didn't complete them, there was a cloud of shame hanging over my head. Growing up practicing "religion" filled me with a sense of dread toward God. I felt that regardless of how much "good" I did, I was still not good enough. In my line of work, as a clinical therapist, I've encountered thousands of patients. Whether these were my patients or patients of clinicians I oversee at the practice, the one common issue that came up in each of their lives was insecurity. The fear of "not being enough" was rooted so deeply that it often resulted in symptoms of anxiety disorders and clinical depression, along with other mental health-related issues. The problem of insecurity was even prevalent among my Christian patients. As I explored the security need with my patients, I realized that although many of them identified themselves as "children of God," they lacked the assurance that they were secure in God's love. They often viewed God as a distant Father, an angry Father, and, most of all, as a disconnected or a busy Father. As I listened to my patients' stories, I was reminded of how I had once held similar misconceptions of God. I remembered the agony I felt in trying to please a god who was impossible to please, and the mental distress that resulted from carrying the weight of impossible standards on my shoulders. It's a heavy weight. It's an unbearable load.

Over the next chapter, we will go over the different ways we strive to attain our sense of security and the consequences that result from our striving.

CHAPTER 3

My Striving for Security

How we attempt to meet our need for security looks different depending on the stage of life we're in. For example: during our toddler years, walking around with a safety blanket or a teddy bear makes us feel secure in our environment. During our childhood years, holding a parent's hand while going down the stairs satisfies this need. As we grow up, calling our "person" during a crisis is a way we attempt to feel secure. Regardless of the method you use, your childhood experiences have likely shaped the way you currently seek your sense of security. Here is why: during the first five years of your life, your brain is like a sponge that absorbs information from the outside world. Your brain then stores this information in a container called your subconscious mind. Throughout your life, your brain pulls information from that container to help you make decisions that will help you attain and sustain your sense of security. Even if we had a healthy childhood, in which we felt our parents were attentive and great providers, the fact remains that we live in a sinful world; therefore we are bound to run into hurts, aches, and pains. I've noticed throughout my life and my patients' lives that, in times of difficulty, it is not within our nature to seek our sense of security from God. In fact, when we experience problems, we tend to employ what mental health professionals call *defense mechanisms*. This term is a fancy way to describe how we approach resolving a problem that we perceive as a threat to our sense of security. When we feel threatened, we tend to rely on information that we stored in our subconscious mind during the first five years of life to resolve today's issues, and when this doesn't work—which it often doesn't—we become very frustrated with ourselves, with others, and with God.

Our defense mechanisms often lead us to search for different outlets to draw security from. For the sake of simplicity, I'm going to refer to these outlets as dead ends, because they lead us nowhere. These dead ends may provide us with security in the short term, but when relied upon long term, they fail to stand the test of time. So we find ourselves going around the same mountain over and over again. Getting your sense of security from a dead end is the cause of many mental health-related issues, including depression and anxiety. Throughout the next few pages, we're going to explore the three most used dead ends of attaining security. As you read through each dead end, I'd like to encourage you to identify which one you find yourself predominantly relying on for your security. I invite you to pray this prayer before you begin:

> Heavenly Father, You are the ultimate provider. Father, I confess that there have been times when I sought to get my sense of security fulfilled apart from you. As I go through the next few sections, please show me where I am currently seeking to fulfill my sense of security independent of you, and help me to seek you first. Amen.

Money

One of the most misused Bible verses is found in 1 Tim 6:10. People often misquote this verse to convey that God views money as evil. In reality, when used in its proper context, 1 Tim 6:10 says: "For the love of money is a root of all kinds of evil. Some people, eager for money, have wandered from the faith and pierced themselves with many griefs." Before we jump into what the Bible is saying in the above passage, let me clarify what God isn't saying. 1) God is not saying that he doesn't want you to have money. 2) God is not saying that you need to hate money. If I could summarize 1 Tim 6:10, it would be this: "Your life is worth more than the materials in this world. Your soul will outlast this life. Therefore, don't let the pursuit of financial success distract you from what God is offering you: eternal life with him." Does God choose to bless people financially? Absolutely! The Bible is filled with passages about people that God chose to bless financially. Take a look at the following passages.

> Abram had become very wealthy in livestock and in silver and gold. (Gen 13:2)

> Isaac planted crops in that land and the same year reaped a hundredfold, because the LORD blessed him. The man became rich, and his wealth continued to grow until he became very wealthy. (Gen 26:12–13)

> "The land is still ours, because we have sought the LORD our God; we sought him and he has given us rest on every side." So they built and prospered. (2 Chron 14:7b, referring to Asa)

I could go on and on. The point is, God isn't against you having money; God is against money having you. No amount of money in the world can grant you the security that God extends to you as his child.

Self

Science has shown through centuries of research that our need for security is met in an environment in which we feel protected and connected simultaneously. In other words, by design we seek to meet our need for security in someone we esteem as powerful enough to protect us and who genuinely has our best interest at heart—neither of which the "god" I believed in provided. My upbringing taught me to view God as both distant and angry. I was taught that God was not approachable. Ever since I was little, I viewed God as a "puppet master" who required blind obedience without a relationship. I viewed God as a dictator, which quite frankly scared me. In an attempt to earn God's favor or be on his good side, I tried my hardest to be "good" and do good things to maybe prove myself worthy enough. I served him out of fear. My attempts lasted only a short while before I grew resentful of God's standards. I felt ashamed for resenting God. Then I was right back to trying to earn my way back into his good graces again. I knew that I needed God for survival per se, but I didn't trust him with my day-to-day decisions, so I tried to figure out every possible way to minimize the amount of dependence I had on God so I wouldn't need him as much. The best way to describe this is like a child who is living in an abusive home. The child knows that he or she needs the abusive parent for "survival," but the child does everything possible to stay out of the abusive parent's way or cause any sort of friction, and hopefully go unnoticed. Self-reliance is a trait that is often derived from *betrayal trauma*. Betrayal trauma is a type of emotional wound that comes from experiences like neglect, abuse, or betrayal inflicted by people who failed to protect us when we relied on them. As a result of this wound, you made an internal vow to yourself to not depend on anyone ever again. That was my life motto for a long time. Many of us have a painful story that leads back to when "self-reliance" began. In my seeking God, he showed me that my self-reliance dated back to betrayals I experienced at a young age. If this section resonates with you, no worries, in the coming chapters, we will go over practical ways to resolve this issue.

People

As I described earlier, when Adam and Eve sinned, they lost their sense of connection with God. Ever since then, humanity has been trying to fill that need. The most common way we tend to approach our need for security is by relying on people. On the surface, relying on others for security satisfies two needs, safety and belonging, simultaneously; however, since the person we tend to rely on is not God, and can never be God, it's only a matter of time before the person falters. When they do, our sense of security comes crumbling down. We feel anxious and depressed.

To better explain this faulty process, take a look at the illustration below: John relies on Jane for his sense of security. One day, Jane is having a bad day and offers no comfort to John. This results in John feeling anxious because his sense of security is now depleted.

Does this sound familiar? I've treated so many people whose emotional highs and lows were a direct reflection of their source of security's emotions. Countless patients have come to see me, convinced that they were suffering from either bipolar disorder or borderline personality disorder because of the intensity of their emotional fluctuations, when in reality, their issue was a result of putting their sense of security in the wrong person.

Here is an example of a patient I once treated: My patient came in for her assessment determined that she met the criteria to be diagnosed with borderline personality disorder, a disorder that is deemed very difficult to treat by mental health professionals. As I listened to her story, it was clear that ever since she was a little girl, my patient put her sense of security in her mom. We are supposed to rely on our parents at a young age. However, as we grow up, our parents' job is to teach us to wean off of them as our main source of security and to rely on God for it. My patient wasn't taught this. So even in her late thirties, she sought her mom's affirmations for most of life's important decisions. I noticed that on the weeks she was sad, she and her mom had had a disagreement; and on the weeks she was happy, she and her mom were on good terms.

The way to break this cycle was not to tell my patient "Don't ask your mom's advice anymore." That could be scary and cause her further anxiety. If this story resonates with you, take heart! We will go over practical steps to resolve this issue in the coming chapters.

Chapter 4

Finding Security in God

Throughout this chapter, I'm going to teach you how to begin developing a sense of security that is 1) stable over time and 2) enduring, regardless of your circumstances. Before I begin teaching you about why God is the source of our security, I'd like to share a little bit about my spiritual background, along with the misconceptions I held about God.

Growing up in an Islamic household, the "god" of my understanding held attributes that made him cruel and unapproachable. Throughout the years, I believed that Allah was the real God.

When I came to faith in Christ, I wish I could tell you that someone waved a magic wand and I immediately trusted that God was safe. On the contrary, when I came to faith in Jesus, I basically transferred the attributes I held of Allah to God. So, although I intellectually believed that Jesus was the risen Son of God and surrendered my life to him, I found myself scared of my new Father God. As a new believer in Jesus, my understanding of God was a mixture of how I viewed Allah plus my experiences with authority figures growing up. In my case, this equated to a God who was mean and distant. Throughout the years as a therapist, I've used the following formula with my patients to help them determine their current view of God and where their view stems from:

my understanding of God during childhood + my relationship with caregivers as a child = my current view of God

Depending on your upbringing, exploring the idea of surrendering to a God you don't know or a God you perceive as mean or untrustworthy is a scary thing. So I commend you for sticking with me to this point. The idea of surrender is also painful if you grew up in an abusive environment or an oppressive environment, where you were mistreated by the person who was supposed to take care of you.

For me, because I had experienced my share of betrayals by authority figures, the idea of surrendering my life to God was a terrifying step. I felt like surrendering my life to Jesus meant that I had to become a "robot." I thought it meant that I would have to resign myself and act like I didn't have feelings, or that my feelings didn't matter. Before I truly got to know God, the thought of "surrendering my life" to him was so triggering, it brought on flashbacks from childhood, where my sense of security was nonexistent.

You see, I didn't doubt God's sovereignty. I knew that God was able. What I doubted was God's goodness and the assurance of his love for me. I viewed God as harsh. So, my relationship with him was transactional, meaning if I was well-behaved, went to church, tithed, and was in the choir, I was safe with God. For years, I believed that God's goodness toward me was contingent on my good behavior. So, I walked around scared of losing his love because of yesterday's sins. I thought I was alone in feeling like this. In fact, I shied away from sharing my true feelings about my fear of God. I put on a brave face in front of everyone, but on the inside, fear and anxiety ate at me.

Fast-forward to years later, I received my license as a counselor. In my line of work, I was privileged to hear people's stories and walk with them through difficult experiences. As I listened to one person after another, it became evident that I wasn't the only one who held the wrong view of God. I'd say 95 percent of the patients I treated had a warped understanding of God. They saw God as either harsh, distant, or both—neither of which made them want to approach God, much less surrender to him and develop a relationship with him. I've found that the lack of understanding of God's true character is the most common reason that keeps people from developing a relationship with God. So, when we hold the wrong perspective of God, we are essentially running from the very Person we need to make us feel whole!

As I mentioned earlier, your upbringing matters so much! In treating my patients, I put a great emphasis on exploring the belief system that was ingrained in them during their childhood years. I've treated patients who were clinically depressed, clinically anxious, and who had experienced severe trauma in their lifetime, along with patients who battled with other mental health disorders. What I found was those who identified themselves as Christians experienced the same torment as those who identified themselves as atheists. As I looked further into this, I realized that regardless of whether you identify yourself as a Christian or not, if you don't hold the correct perspective of God's sovereignty and God's goodness in your life, you will have trouble defeating anxiety, depression, trauma, and other mental health-related disorders. The outer label of "Christian" doesn't matter if your day-to-day relationship with God is nonexistent. I found this to be true in my life. I found it to be true in my patients' lives. And I truly believe with all my heart that this is true for you as well.

The key element that made the difference between a patient who did not overcome mental health issues and a patient who did was whether my patient chose to have an active, personal relationship with God as their heavenly Father. My patients who developed a trusting relationship with God as their heavenly Father experienced such a decrease in their symptoms that they were no longer considered clinically depressed or clinically anxious.

Throughout the next chapter, I'm going to teach you how to develop a secure relationship with God as your heavenly Father. To do so, you must understand that God is both sovereign and good, simultaneously. Believing that God is sovereign yet not good will make him seem unapproachable and thus cause you to seek safety elsewhere. Conversely, if you believe that God is good and not sovereign, you will doubt his true ability to protect you from harm and thus seek safety elsewhere. Let's explore this further:

The God Who Is Sovereign but Not Good

As I mentioned earlier, your upbringing directly influences how you view God. If you view God as sovereign and powerful, yet lacking in goodness, one or more of the following terms will likely resonate with you (*please circle how you view God currently, not how you'd like to view him*):

- God is controlling.
- God is looking down on me, waiting for me to mess up.
- God is impatient.
- God is on his last straw with me.
- God is mad at me.
- God doesn't like me because of what I've done.
- God could care less about me.
- God has better things to think about/do than to care for me.

If the descriptions above fit your view of God on any level, then you may find yourself apprehensive about developing a relationship with him. Believing that God is sovereign, yet lacking in goodness, is one of the most common and dangerous misconceptions we can hold about God. Doubting God's goodness creates an inner turmoil within us that causes us to make fear-based and anxiety-driven decisions. A prime example of someone who viewed God as sovereign yet not good is found in Matt 25. The parable tells of a master, who in this story represents God, who distributes an indicated number of talents (units of money) to three people. The master comes back later to collect a return on his investments. The first two people represent those who trust in

God's sovereignty and his goodness simultaneously. They had put their talents to good use and doubled their investments for their master. The third person, however, reflects someone who views his master as powerful yet lacking in goodness. Look at his response in Matt 25:24–25: "Then the man who had received one bag of gold came. 'Master,' he said, 'I knew that you are a hard man, harvesting where you have not sown and gathering where you have not scattered seed. So I was afraid and went out and hid your gold in the ground. See, here is what belongs to you.'" You can tell how he views his master (God) from his response. Take a look at what happened next: "His master replied, 'You wicked, lazy servant! So you knew that I harvest where I have not sown and gather where I have not scattered seed?'" (Matt 25:26). Just to clarify, the master is not confirming that he is indeed harsh. He is responding according to the comments the servant made about him. The master continued: "Well then, you should have put my money on deposit with the bankers, so that when I returned I would have received it back with interest" (Matt 25:27). We see from this parable that the servant's incorrect view of God caused him to become paralyzed with fear and anxiety, to the point where he literally failed to accomplish what God had intended for him. Isn't this what often happens to us? We think that God is for others but not for us. We view God as harsh or uncaring, yet wonder why we live with such paralyzing anxiety and debilitating fears. Holding God's character in contempt, or viewing him as sovereign yet not good, is one of the main causes of anxiety and depression. I attest to this from my personal life and the lives of the patients I've treated. When we don't trust in God's goodness, we will doubt that he has our best interest at heart and end up in a space where we feel like we must face giant problems on our own.

The God Who Is Good but Not Sovereign

There are times when we adopt a view of God that acknowledges his goodness but without acknowledging his sovereignty. There is no greater example of God's goodness than the finished work of the cross. But if we fail to acknowledge the reason Jesus had to go to the cross, then we fail to acknowledge the true nature of God's holiness and his sovereignty. If you view God as good and loving, yet lacking in sovereignty, one or more of the following terms will likely resonate with you (*please circle how you view God currently, not how you'd like to view him*):

- God doesn't have control over everything.

- God has bigger fish to fry.

- My parents didn't care about me, why should God?

- God doesn't hear my prayers.

- If God is so powerful, then why didn't my prayers get answered?

- God listens only to the prayers of ministers.

- God is too busy for me.

If you circled any of the descriptions above, I can see why you would be apprehensive about developing a relationship with God. Like I mentioned before, we look for security in a person we esteem as sovereign and good. The reality is, God is sovereign over everything. We may not understand the reason he allows things to happen, but that doesn't mean that they happened outside of his control.

A great example of God's sovereignty is found in the book of Jonah. Take a look at the following passage: "The word of the Lord came to Jonah son of Amittai: 'Go to the great city of Nineveh and preach against it, because its wickedness has come up before me.' But Jonah ran away from the Lord and headed for Tarshish. He went down to Joppa, where he found a ship bound for that port. After paying the fare, he went aboard and sailed for Tarshish to flee from the Lord" (Jonah 1:1).

Here we see that God tells Jonah to go preach a message. Jonah shows utter contempt for God's command by running away from him. Here is how God responds to Jonah's disobedience: "Then the Lord sent a great wind on the sea, and such a violent storm arose that the ship threatened to break up. All the sailors were afraid and each cried out to his own god. And they threw the cargo into the sea to lighten the ship." Here we find all the sailors in despair, trying to remedy the situation by crying out to their own "gods." Meanwhile, "Jonah had gone below deck, where he lay down and fell into a deep sleep. The captain went to him and said, "How can you sleep? Get up and call on your god! Maybe he will take notice of us so that we will not perish" (Jonah 1:4–6). So the sailors inquired of Jonah's identity. The Bible says: "He answered, 'I am a Hebrew and I worship the LORD, the God of heaven, who made the sea and the dry land'" (Jonah 1:9). It's interesting that Jonah identified himself with God's chosen people and acknowledged God's sovereignty, yet the reason he was on that boat was out of contempt for God's command. When the storm continued to rage, Jonah finally conceded to the fact that God is God and Jonah is not God. In his guilt, Jonah encouraged the people to throw him off the boat in order to save their own lives. When they did, we see God's sovereignty yet again in Jonah's life. The Bible says: "Now the LORD provided a huge fish to swallow Jonah, and Jonah was in the belly of the fish three days and three nights" (Jonah 1:17). Then Jonah prayed a prayer of repentance and vowed to do as God asked. As soon as Jonah finished praying, the Bible says: "And the LORD commanded the fish, and it vomited Jonah onto dry land" (Jonah 2:10).

The story continues in Jonah 3:1–2: "Then the word of the LORD came to Jonah a second time: 'Go to the great city of Nineveh and proclaim to it the message I give you.'" This time, Jonah obeyed God by telling the city to repent, and the people of Nineveh repented right away. How did Jonah respond? God's mercy toward the city of Nineveh made Jonah mad. Jonah felt upset that God was good to the people of Nineveh. Look at Jonah's conversation with God: "He prayed to the LORD, 'Isn't this what I said, LORD, when I was still at home? That is what I tried to forestall by fleeing to Tarshish. I knew that you are a gracious and compassionate God, slow to anger and abounding in love, a God who relents from sending calamity'" (Jonah 4:2). You see, Jonah was very aware of God's goodness, but he lacked reverence for God's sovereignty on this matter. He must have thought that if he fled, then the people of Nineveh "would get what they deserved." Isn't that how we act sometimes? It's clear from God's word that Jonah was comfortable with expressing his feelings to God. The Bible recorded instances in which God instigated a conversation with Jonah to further explore Jonah's emotions. To drive the point of his sovereignty home, while Jonah was sitting down waiting to watch the fate of the people of Nineveh, God provided a plant to shield Jonah from the sun. The next day, God allowed for the plant to wither. Jonah became upset. God in his infinite wisdom used this moment to reveal to Jonah the depth of God's compassion. Take a look at the following conversation between God and Jonah: "But God said to Jonah, 'Is it right for you to be angry about the plant?' 'It is,' he [Jonah] said. 'And I'm so angry I wish I were dead.' But the LORD said, 'You have been concerned about this plant, though you did not tend it or make it grow. It sprang up overnight and died overnight. And should I not have concern for the great city of Nineveh, in which there are more than a hundred and twenty thousand people who cannot tell their right hand from their left—and also many animals?'" (Jonah 4:9–11).

The book of Jonah is only one example that displays the sovereignty of God over all of his creation: the wind, the sea, the fish, man's life, etc. When we don't hold the proper understanding of God's sovereignty, we will likely fall into the trap of viewing God as a "genie in a bottle." This view is dangerous because it gives us a false sense of security in our relationship with God. We start to view God as someone who is here to make our desires a reality. And when that does not happen, we get mad at him and grow resentful toward him. Having the proper understanding of God's sovereignty means respecting God's position as God—which also means knowing that he is God and we are not. This is the point that God drove home in Jonah's life: that his goodness doesn't negate his sovereignty, and vice versa. Although God disciplined Jonah for disobeying his command, God still reflected his goodness in rescuing Jonah. While we must revere God, we mustn't forget that acknowledging God's holiness is scary only if we have not trusted in the finished work of the cross. Because in Jesus, we can approach God as both our God and our Father.

The Good and Sovereign God

The Bible is filled with examples that reflect God's goodness and sovereignty simultaneously. Our need to understand the Person of God from both perspectives simultaneously is crucial to our ability to stand on the security of God's love when facing life's difficulties. Look at King Hezekiah, for example. The Bible records that from his early life, "he held fast to the LORD and did not stop following him; he kept the commands the LORD had given Moses. And the LORD was with him; he was successful in whatever he undertook" (2 Kgs 18:6–7a). As a king over God's people, Hezekiah used his influence to draw people back to God: "If you return to the LORD, then your fellow Israelites and your children will be shown compassion by their captors and will return to this land, for the Lord your God is gracious and compassionate. He will not turn his face from you if you return to him" (2 Chron 30:9). Throughout his reign, King Hezekiah interceded for those God placed under his authority: "May the LORD, who is good, pardon everyone" (2 Chron 30:18b). His prayers often reflected his faith in God's goodness and sovereignty, and we see God's response as follows: "And the LORD heard Hezekiah and healed the people" (2 Chron 30:20). Even when faced with a national crisis, King Hezekiah stood firm in his faith and encouraged people to do the same: "'Be strong and courageous. Do not be afraid or discouraged because of the king of Assyria and the vast army with him, for there is a greater power with us than with him. With him is only the arm of flesh, but with us is the LORD our God to help us and to fight our battles.' And the people gained confidence from what Hezekiah the king of Judah said" (2 Chron 32:7–8).

We can see from King Hezekiah's life that his faith in God was built on the foundation of God's unshakable character. When faced with a crisis that would have caused most of us to cave in with anxiety, depression, and inconsolable grief, King Hezekiah looked to the only One who could bring deliverance and said: "Now, Lord our God, deliver us from his hand, so that all the kingdoms of the earth may know that you alone, Lord, are God" (2 Kgs 19:19). The following verse says: "Then Isaiah son of Amoz sent a message to Hezekiah: 'This is what the Lord, the God of Israel, says: I have heard your prayer concerning Sennacherib king of Assyria'" (2 Kgs 19:20). God's answer was followed by God's deliverance.

As you can see from Hezekiah's life, God's sovereignty and his goodness are two sides of the same coin. I don't want you to wait until a crisis hits to try to get to know him. Throughout the next few chapters, we're going to dive into God's characteristics, to help you get more comfortable with the only One who is able to deliver you from anxiety, depression, past traumas, grief, and more! My prayer is that as you get to know him, his goodness, and his sovereignty, you will feel the grip of anxiety and depression loosen from you and his love take hold of you.

Chapter 5

Getting to Know God

It's hard to put your trust in someone you don't know. Think about it: if you were looking up a surgeon who would perform heart surgery on you or on a loved one, you'd likely conduct a lot of research to make sure the surgeon was credible. The process of getting to know God is similar. Through Scripture, you begin to learn about God, his character, and his attributes. And just like you'd not only make sure that the surgeon was credible through research, you'd also want to meet with the surgeon to make sure they knew what they were talking about. Developing a relationship with God works in a similar way. It is through meeting with him and walking with him that we are able to experience his faithfulness, enabling us to develop a secure trust in him.

Let's say years later you have a friend who needs a similar surgery. You would then be able to recommend that surgeon to your friend because of the historical experience you had had with the surgeon. In the same way, you'd be willing to recommend God to those who are in need of hope.

As you gain history in your walk with God, you begin to trust in his attributes, and see for yourself that God is who he says he is, regardless of your childhood background. As you continue to walk with God, your level of trust in him will supersede the negative concepts you held of him. The Bible says, "For the word of God is alive and active. Sharper than any double-edged sword, it penetrates even to dividing soul and spirit, joints and marrow; it judges the thoughts and attitudes of the heart" (Heb 4:12). This means that God's word has the power to reveal to you the lies you've held about yourself and the lies you've held about him. That, my friends, is the truth that has the power to transform you and guide you toward freedom from anxiety, depression, and more!

Again, this process cannot be reduced to giving a hurting person who doesn't have a relationship with God one or two Bible verses, without putting an emphasis on developing a relationship with God. The journey of healing and developing a relationship with God that is based on trust to meet our need for security is a process. Developing a solid foundation with God as your heavenly Father, as your Savior, and your Redeemer will take time, but I promise you that this relationship is your best line of defense against clinical depression, anxiety, and other forms of mental health-related issues. Putting your trust in the goodness and the sovereignty of God will be the best investment you will ever make in your life.

Just like you'd need to get to know a person before you felt comfortable developing a relationship with him or her, we're going to start with getting to know God through his word.

The Bible says: "God is love" (1 John 4:8b). To describe God's love, the Bible says, "Such love has no fear, because perfect love expels all fear. If we are afraid, it is for fear of punishment, and this shows that we have not fully experienced his perfect love" (1 John 4:18 NLT).

Describe a time when you were afraid of God's punishment (we've all been there!):

____

____

____

Now, go back to 1 John 4:18, and write down what this verse says about the way you are to relate to God:

____

____

____

Scripture also says: "The fear of the LORD is the beginning of wisdom, and knowledge of the Holy One is understanding" (Prov 9:10).

"Whoa. Wait a minute!" you might say. "If God is love, and his perfect love expels fear, how is the fear of God the beginning of wisdom?"

Great question! Here is the answer: fear here is used in the context of reverence. The above Bible verse means that the only one worthy of our reverence is God. A wise person by biblical definition is a person who acknowledges that the only One who belongs on the throne of his or her life is God. "The fear of the Lord" doesn't mean you need to hide from God. It means acknowledging that God alone is worthy of worship. "The fear of the Lord" refers to you acknowledging that although you may respect your mom and dad, your spouse, grandparents, employer, and whoever else, your greatest reverence must be reserved for God alone.

As we explore God's characteristics further, I pray "that the God of our Lord Jesus Christ, the glorious Father, may give you the Spirit of wisdom and revelation, so that you may know him better. I pray that the eyes of your heart may be enlightened in order that you may know the hope to which he has called you" (Eph 1:17–18a). Let's get started!

God Is Patient

When we are the recipient of someone's patience toward us, we're likely to let our guard down and draw closer to the person. We are also more likely to share vulnerabilities with the person who has demonstrated patience with us than we are with someone who gets on our case every time we mess up!

One of my greatest concerns in my relationship with God was that his patience was running thinner with me with every one of my mishaps. Have you ever felt like you are one mishap away from God abandoning you? That's one of the most common beliefs my patients expressed during therapy. My patients were convinced that God's patience toward them had run out and that they were "too far gone" for God to love them. To that I would respond, "His love for you is greater than your mistakes!" This doesn't mean that God won't hold us to a standard. The Bible says, "Do not conform to the pattern of this world, but be transformed by the renewing of your mind" (Rom 12:2a). This transformation will look much like this: "When I was a child, I talked like a child, I thought like a child, I reasoned like a child. When I became a man, I put the ways of childhood behind me" (1 Cor 13:11).

Just like I would hold my twelve-year-old to a higher standard than when he or she was six years old, as you walk with God and grow in Christ, you will begin to see that things you used to do that didn't bother you now bother you. My husband and I like to use this example to describe my progression in my walk with the Lord: it wasn't until five years after I started walking with Jesus that I started putting the grocery cart back where it belongs. I know! It's terrible. But seriously, for years, even as a Christian, I didn't—and it didn't bother me, until one day it did, and I have put it back ever since!

I've met so many people who have been afraid to draw close to God out of fear that he will expose everything they need to fix before he accepts them. That's a lie from the pit of hell. God accepts you as you are when you surrender your life to him. Out of your surrender, he begins to work with you and in you, little by little. All you need to do is draw close to him and trust him. And when you mess up, do not run from God. Instead, draw close to him. God will not throw in the towel on you. On the contrary, God will hold on to you even when you're ready to give up on yourself. His patience sustains you when you feel like you have yet again messed up and are not worthy of one more chance. His patience with you shows you that he is for you, and if you look over and there's nobody cheering for you, just know that he is. He has had your best interest at heart, as the Bible says, "He is patient with you, not wanting anyone to perish, but everyone to come to repentance" (2 Pet 3:9b). God knows that an outward appearance of change doesn't last; that's why he's after your heart. When you begin to see yourself the way God sees you in Christ, your behavior will naturally start to follow.

Growing in our understanding of God's patience toward us is also a reminder for us to be patient with those who are not as strong in the faith as we are, and instead of passing judgment on people or gossiping about them or condemning them, may we pray for them. I'm not saying we shouldn't hold our brothers and sisters in Christ accountable. There's a difference between holding someone accountable and holding someone in judgment. Accountability says, "Hey, you're better than this!" Judgment says "Hey, I'm better than you!" My friends, the Bible warns us about comparing ourselves to other people, or comparing our walk with theirs. Take a look at Gal 6:4–5: "Each one should test their own actions. Then they can take pride in themselves alone, without comparing themselves to someone else, for each one should carry their own load."

In summary, God's patience is for the purpose of our redemption. Each one of us has been given an assignment according to God's will, plans, and purposes. We are to reflect God's patience for the purpose of encouraging our brothers and sisters in Christ in their walk with him.

A Question to Ponder

In what way has God been patient with me over the last year?

____

____

____

God Is Kind

Throughout his years on earth, Jesus reflected God's heart to mankind. One of my favorite Bible passages that exemplifies this is John 7:53—8:11. In this passage, Jesus was faced with a woman who was about to be stoned for committing adultery, in accordance with the Mosaic law. As her accusers were shaming her, the only One who was worthy of condemning her—didn't. Instead of joining the accusers in condemnation, his kindness was revealed in his response to her in John 8:10–11: "Jesus straightened up and asked her, 'Woman, where are they? Has no one condemned you?' 'No one, sir,' she said. 'Then neither do I condemn you,' Jesus declared. 'Go now and leave your life of sin.'"

Has anyone ever tried to motivate you to do something by shaming you or using other negative motivation techniques? Negative reinforcement doesn't produce lasting change because it results in striving that is motivated by some kind of fear, whether it's fear of rejection or fear of failure, etc. Although negative reinforcement may result in "good behavior" in the short term, it deals only with the symptoms rather than the root of the issue. Take a look at the historical patterns of behavior the Israelites were stuck in. One generation behaved according to the law, and then two generations worshiped idols; then the next generation came after them, repented, and committed themselves to God; then the next generation fell backwards again. I'm not saying that rules are bad. Obviously, rules were meant to keep us within the guardrails that God has set for us, and often for our safety. For example, there's a reason we're not supposed to cross the street when the light is green. However, generally, when our primary motivation to adhere to the rules is fear, our adherence doesn't produce an internal change. Here is why: our brain has a paired structure called the amygdala. Think of the amygdala as a house that is filled with rooms; each room contains an emotion, like happiness, fear, excitement, etc. Depending on what's going on in your life, the amygdala signals which emotion you should feel. For example, when you're getting ready to go on your first date, the amygdala signals "excitement" to light up, so you feel excited.

The problem with the amygdala is that it tends to pull from information that was fed to us growing up. So for example, if you grew up with the belief that God is an angry authoritarian figure, you will walk around believing that God is angry with you instead of believing that God is looking at you with kindness. When we walk around believing that God is angry with us, we soon find ourselves carrying a burden that is too heavy to bear. So we end up reacting in one of two ways:

1. We will try to work hard to gain God's favor, and since effort doesn't come close to God's standard, when we mess up, we will beat ourselves up and get angry with ourselves, which will result in depression. This type of depression comes from unprocessed anger toward self for failing to meet a standard that is too high for you to meet.

2. After we beat ourselves up long enough, some of us make the conscious decision to walk away from God. We end up living with a ton of anxiety because we are putting most of our energy into keeping our guard up.

Whichever way resonates with you the most, God is inviting you to lay your burdens down and let him take care of you. Jesus said: "Come to me, all you who are weary and burdened, and I will give you rest. Take my yoke upon you and learn from me, for I am gentle and humble in heart, and you will find rest for your souls. For my yoke is easy and my burden is light" (Matt 11:28–30). Jesus is inviting you to lay your "works" down, to lay your guard down, to lay your striving down, and find rest in the fact that he has already met the standard for you, so that in him, you can find rest for your soul in knowing that you are secure in his love. When you truly know how much God loves you, how secure you are in his arms, and how much he yearns to lavish you with his love, you will feel at peace, and you will find a rest that will produce internal change in you. You will no longer feel the need to strive to earn

God's love; instead, you will live and act as a secure child of God, and his love will overflow in different parts of your life.

Looking from the outside, it's often easy for us to spot the difference between a secure and an insecure child. For example, when my daughter was born, my son went through a period of time when his behavior regressed. For a couple of weeks, it was evident that he questioned the love his father and I had for him, because up until this point, he had been our only child, and so our full attention had been on him. Then his sister came along, and our attention became divided. It was evident that my son felt displaced. It took a couple of weeks for him to realize that "Mommy and Daddy still love me just as much; I just have a playmate now," and life went on. But believe me when I tell you, it took intentional and conscious effort to make sure he knew that he was not replaced and that he was just as much of a vital part of our family as he was before his sister came along.

An adult example of this is found in the response of the older brother in the parable of the prodigal son. When the prodigal son returned and the father received him with compassion, the Bible says that the older brother was upset with the father's kindness toward the younger brother: "The older brother became angry and refused to go in. So his father went out and pleaded with him. But he answered his father, 'Look! All these years I've been slaving for you and never disobeyed your orders. Yet you never gave me even a young goat so I could celebrate with my friends. But when this son of yours who has squandered your property with prostitutes comes home, you kill the fattened calf for him!'" (Luke 15:28–30). As you can see, the older brother had been insecure in his relationship with his father, and so he spent years striving to be the "good kid." How often do we get caught in this cycle of striving to earn God's favor, or worse, the favor of those who don't even feel secure in themselves.

God's word says, "For God gave us a spirit not of fear but of power and love and self-control" (2 Tim 1:7 ESV). In order to lead a lifestyle marked by power, love, and self-control, we have to master our emotions. When we learn to control our emotions, we grow in our ability to reason. Our ability to reason comes from the prefrontal cortex. This is the part of our brain that controls decision-making. The way God made us, we can't operate out of two places of our brain at the same time. So we can either react out of emotion or respond out of reasoning. Take a look below:

Reacting Out of Fear	Responding Out of Reasoning
Is God against me?	God is for me (see Rom 8:31).
I don't feel God!	God is with me (see Ps 16:8).
Did God abandon me?	God will never leave me or forsake me (see Deut 31:6).
God must have turned his back on me!	God is pursuing me (see John 1:11–13).

In order for us to develop the ability to respond wisely, we have to be at the point where we are resting in the security of God's love for us. So in order for your emotions to calm down, you have to rest in God's love. When you anchor yourself to God's love, the emotional part of your brain, the amygdala, literally calms down to the point that it turns its light off, allowing you to make decisions out of the frontal part of your brain—decisions that are not fear induced.

In summary, walking with God and experiencing his love has the power to produce identity-level change, which is far deeper than behavior change. This is the change that enables us to "love because he first loved us" (1 John 4:19), because this love is a decision that comes out of the overflow of God's love for us, regardless of whether the person deserves it or not.

Now, back to the woman caught in the act of adultery. Since Jesus is God and was with the Father when he made us, Jesus knew all about our brain function and how kindness, not shaming, is what produces lasting identity change. Before we look at what Jesus said, let's take a look at what he didn't say. Jesus didn't respond with "Go leave your life of sin, then I won't condemn you." A response like this would have thrown the woman back into the fear-based behavior pattern. Instead, Jesus said: "Then neither do I condemn you. . . . Go now and leave your life of sin" (John 8:11).

In other words, Jesus restored her, and out of that restoration, Jesus gave her the best possible chance of changing her lifestyle.

I want to close this attribute with a reminder from Rom 2:4; that God's kindness is intended to lead you to repentance. If you are not in a relationship with God, he is pursuing you with compassion. If you are in a relationship with him, he is inviting you to a closer and a deeper intimacy with him as your heavenly Father.

A Question to Ponder

How has God shown me kindness throughout the past year?

____

____

____

God Does Not Envy

Another way of stating this is "God is a giver, not a taker." Envy stems from perceived lack, but God doesn't need anything, because he is self-sufficient. One of the greatest weapons of deception the enemy uses is in persuading you that God wants to take something from you or that God wants to keep something good from you. Genesis 3 unveils how believing this lie caused Eve to question God's character and resulted in Adam and Eve's choice to go against God's command and get kicked out of the garden of Eden.

The same enemy who was at work back then is still at work now. One of the ways your enemy, also known as Satan or "the deceiver," tricks you is by convincing you that God wants to take *something good* from you. The only way to combat this lie is by looking at what God's word says about this matter. This allows us to examine historical evidence within its context.

Before we jump into who God is, let's deal with the three most common questions I've been asked about this attribute.

1. "If God is a giver, why did he not answer my prayer?"

    Trust me, you're not the first person to ask this, and you won't be the last. We've all struggled with this question at one time or another. There have been many times in my life when I've prayed for something and felt like my prayers were just bouncing off the ceiling. For example, my call to follow Jesus included separation from my blood relatives, whom I practically worshiped at one time. There were many times when I was tempted to question why God hadn't given me a better family or a better childhood. Since I was too scared to approach God about this hurt, I denied it, but it kept eating at me. One day, I laid down my guard and cried out to God about it. To my surprise, God didn't strike me down for asking. Instead, he answered. Not in the way I wanted him to, but in a way that brought peace to my heart about the situation.

    There are different accounts in Scripture where God chooses to not answer prayers the way people want him to. A well-known account is recorded by Paul in the Bible. Paul talks about a thorn in his flesh that has been tormenting him. Although we don't know what the "the thorn in the flesh" was, it's clear that it was something that Paul wanted God to take away from him, as recorded in 2 Cor 12:8–9: "Three times I pleaded with the Lord to take it away from me. But he said to me, 'My grace is sufficient for you, for my power is made perfect in weakness.' Therefore I will boast all the more gladly about my weaknesses, so that Christ's power may rest on me." As you petition God for your desires, I'd like to encourage you to remember that God sees what you don't see. He knows what you don't know. Whether it's an engagement that didn't work out or a business deal that fell through, remember, God's will is for your best interest!

2. "If God is a giver, why does his call require me to surrender my life to him?"

    This life is not your final destination. Regardless of how great life may seem, what Jesus offers you is greater: eternal life with him. "Can't I have both?" you may ask. To which I'd answer: "Jesus wants to be number one in your life." There isn't room for God plus (another object of worship—whether social media, family, kids, etc.). So the call to surrender your life to Jesus is a call to reprioritize your life according to what he wants for you. This can happen only when you truly grasp how much it cost God to redeem you. Only then you're able to say: "I have been crucified with Christ and I no longer live, but Christ lives in me. The life I now live in the body, I live by faith in the Son of God, who loved me and gave himself for me" (Gal 2:20).

3. "If God is a giver, why does the call to follow him come at all costs?"

Plain and simple, our nature is self-destructive. Without God, we get ourselves into trouble, whether by our own doing or by someone else's doing. We were created for worship, and if God is not first in our lives, we will worship something or someone else, whether that be our spouse, our kids, sports, social media, etc. God wants to be the Person we worship. He made us. He loves us more than anyone else can ever love us. He is the only Person who was able and willing to give us eternal life with him. There are no God-substitutes. God may use people or things as a vessel of his provision for you, but make no mistake, he is the source of your provision.

I can tell you story after story to encourage your faith in God's provision. My personal favorite is of the time when God called me down to Myrtle Beach. Following Jesus meant cutting ties with family, job, home, and lifestyle. I moved to Myrtle Beach with nothing but the call of God on my life and found out that the job I had lined up fell through. So I was back at square one, looking for a job. I found a job and was invited to church by my co-workers. I surrendered my life to Christ. The peace I remember feeling in the days that followed was beyond my understanding, considering I was in a position where I had no place to live and was behind on my car payments, with the bank threatening to repossess my car. I was at the point where I had nothing of material value, yet

I had everything I was looking for. I had nothing from an earthly perspective, yet I had inherited everything of value: everlasting life with my heavenly Father. God was faithful to me. One Sunday morning, I went to church not knowing where my next meal would come from. I met a lady who said she felt that I needed a place to stay. Whoa! Was God at work or what? I didn't accept the invitation right away because my guard was up. I thanked the lady after the church service, we exchanged phone numbers, and I drove to McDonald's to get lunch. Once I got to the McDonald's parking lot, I realized that I didn't have enough money to buy a meal. So, I humbly called the lady I had met at church and asked if she was serious about me staying with her. She said, "Yes! Come on over." In one day, I went from not having a home to sleeping on a memory foam mattress in a home where everything was provided for me. I hadn't worked for it. I hadn't earned it. That's how God works. Whatever God is calling you to put down, I promise that what he has for you is better. God wants your heart. Give him your heart, and watch what he does with your life!

A Question to Ponder

In what way has God provided for me in the past three years?

____

____

____

God Does Not Boast

We all know people who like to show off their achievements, whether on social media or at the dinner table. People who brag about how many degrees they hold or the people they know, as a way of proving their worth. You see, God doesn't need to boast, because he is God. He created everything, and he holds ultimate power over everything. There were instances in the Bible where God reminded people of his power as a way of reassuring them to keep their eyes on him and not on their problems. When we experience fear, we are wired to seek protection from a source that we perceive is more powerful than us. If you're a parent, think back to your child's first day at school or when your child meets a stranger for the first time. It's typical for a child to cling to the parent or to an attachment figure as a way of protecting themselves from perceived danger. This is a protective mechanism that God placed within us to deter us from danger.

Throughout Scripture, we see God demonstrating his power in tangible ways to teach us that he is our source of security. Think about the disciples on the boat during the storm. The disciples panicked as soon as the wind picked up. Isn't that what we do in life? Scripture says that Jesus came walking toward them on water. God will sometimes allow certain issues to come to our lives to strengthen our faith in him. Jesus called out to Peter to walk to him. Peter started walking on water, which is a miracle in itself, but as soon as he took his eyes off of Jesus and looked at the storm, he felt fear and started sinking. Peter felt anxiety when he compared himself to the problem he was facing. In comparison, Peter was no match for the storm; but Jesus was more powerful.

The same principle applies to us: you are not wired to face your problems on your own. This is where most types of anxiety-related disorders originate. You're supposed to seek God to solve your problems. That is when you experience the peace that surpasses understanding.

The remainder of the passage says that Peter cried out, "Lord, save me!" (Matt 14:30). Peter did what we are to do when we're in a rut: cry out to God. What did Jesus do in response to Peter's cry? Scripture says: "Immediately Jesus reached out his hand and caught him" (Matt 14:31a). God wants you and me to cry out to him as our first line of defense, not as our last resort.

Another passage where God displays his power tangibly is Mark 5:25–34. The passage tells about a woman who struggled with bleeding for many years. In that culture, bleeding rendered her unclean. The Bible says that the woman spent all of her money on doctors' appointments in search of a cure, only for her condition to get worse. Then Jesus entered the picture! "When she heard about Jesus, she came up behind him in the crowd and touched his cloak, because she thought, 'If I just touch his clothes, I will be healed.' Immediately her bleeding stopped and she felt in her body that she was freed from her suffering" (Mark 5:27–29). Did Jesus act like she bothered him? No! Jesus responded by commending her faith in front of the crowd. God wants you and me to seek him and to trust in him. Does this mean that we should forget about doctors? Absolutely not! Medicine is a tool that God uses to heal people; however, God wants you to seek him first and to invite him to be a part of your life journey.

Life problems are inevitable. In fact, one of Jesus's exhortations found in John 16:33 says: "I have told you these things, so that in me you may have peace. In this world you will have trouble. But take heart! I have overcome the world." In other words, it's not a matter of if you run into issues; it's when you run into them, here is your solution: look to Jesus first. Compare your problem to him, not to yourself, and when you do, you will experience a peace that makes no sense to the world, a peace that comes only from him, and you will be able to confidently declare: "I keep my eyes always on the LORD. With him at my right hand, I will not be shaken" (Ps 16:8).

A Question to Ponder

What issues am I facing right now that I need to seek God's wisdom on?

____

____

____

God Is Not Proud

Pride is the opposite of humility. Humility is the basis of the gospel. Jesus is the perfect example of someone who reflects perfect humility. This is how the Bible describes Jesus: "Who, being in very nature God, did not consider equality with God something to be used to his own advantage; rather, he made himself nothing by taking the very nature of a servant, being made in human likeness. And being found in appearance as a man, he humbled himself by becoming obedient to death—even death on a cross!" (Phil 2:6–8). Why did Christ willingly go to the cross on our behalf? Because he had our best interest in mind. Pride looks at self-interest; humility looks at the interest of others. Even while he was being crucified and mocked, Jesus said, "Father, forgive them, for they do not know what they are doing" (Luke 23:34a). God's relentless pursuit of our hearts is the perfect reflection of his humility.

Some of my patients expressed worry that God would turn them away or not accept them, because they had met a certain threshold of sin from which they could never come back. Others believed that they needed to clean their lives up before they approached God, because "God certainly wouldn't accept me in my mess." Both mindsets contradict God's nature. In reality, you and I have given God countless reasons to stop pursuing us, yet he continues to choose us! God sees the mess you got yourself in, and he knows that you can't clean it up on your own. So, he invites you to come with your mess and watch how he turns it into a testimony that will bring multitudes to know that he is their Redeemer!

A Question to Ponder

In what ways has God acted in my best interest throughout my life?

____

____

____

God Does Not Dishonor Others

One of the best Bible passages that portrays this characteristic is found in the parable of the prodigal son, in Luke 15:11–32. When the prodigal son returned home, his father was within his right to not receive him back. His father was also within his right to have him work as a servant in his field. After all, the son was the one who chose to dishonor his father, cash out on his inheritance early, and squander his wealth. But this isn't how the story went, is it? The Bible says: "So he got up and went to his father. But while he was still a long way off, his father saw him and was filled with compassion for him; he ran to his son, threw his arms around him and kissed him. The son said to him, 'Father, I have sinned against heaven and against you. I am no longer worthy to be called your son.' But the father said to his servants, 'Quick! Bring the best robe and put it on him. Put a ring on his finger and sandals on his feet. Bring the fattened calf and kill it. Let's have a feast and celebrate. For this son of mine was dead and is alive again; he was lost and is found.' So they began to celebrate" (Luke 15:20–24).

As you see from this parable, the father was eager to restore his son, so much so that he ran toward his son when he saw him coming home. The father received his son with open arms and welcomed him back home. Before the son did anything to deserve his title back as a "son," his father reinstated him. His father celebrated him by having his servants put the "best robe" on him, a ring on his finger, and sandals on his feet—signifying honor to the son who had once dishonored him. This, my friends, is the heart of the Father toward you. We have all dishonored God in one way or another. Yet, in his mercy God chose to redeem us. In his love, Jesus chose to replace our shame with his honor, so that we would be able to stand before him as brothers and sisters in Christ.

A Question to Ponder

Whenever I mess up, do I run from God or do I run toward God and ask him to forgive me?

____

____

____

God Is Not Self-Seeking

The opposite of someone who looks out for themselves is someone who looks out for the interest of others. You know, for years as a believer, I identified Jesus with humility, and God—The Father—with wrath. I viewed Jesus as the "good cop," and God as the "bad cop". You didn't have to convince me that Jesus was loving. After all, he saved me. But I was scared of God. I honestly didn't believe that God loved me. I viewed myself as a plan B. My thought process, though faulty, was: if my parents, who had had the optimal opportunity to love me, didn't, how could God who holds the highest level of honor and glory find it in his heart to love me? On the outside, I looked like the brave, ex-Muslim girl who gave her life to Jesus. On the inside, I was eaten up with fear that God would one day change his mind about me. What would I do then? What would I be left with? I was scared that one day God would realize, "I don't know if she's worth my investment." Or that he would decide, "It would be less work for me to invest in someone who grew up in church." But, friends, that's not the God we serve. Because before the foundations of the world, God thought of you, God thought of me and looked at Jesus and decided to redeem us.

That's what Eph 1 is all about! Take a look: "Even before he made the world, God loved us and chose us in Christ to be holy and without fault in his eyes. God decided in advance to adopt us into his own family by bringing us to himself through Jesus Christ. This is what he wanted to do, and it gave him great pleasure" (Eph 1:4–5 NLT).

A Question to Ponder

As I think about my day-to-day decisions, do I believe that I am more influenced by God's love or by the fear of his wrath toward me?

____

____

____

God Is Not Easily Angered

I grew up with a parent whose temperament was like a pressure cooker. Everything would be fine, and all of a sudden, an eruption would come out of left field, leaving me and those around me walking on eggshells, each of us hoping we were not the ones in the hot seat this time.

My first seven or eight years as a believer, I wasted a lot of time waiting for God's anger to erupt. I had transferred my parent's temperament onto God. Believing that God's wrath was spewed without warning was a scary feeling. It brought on anxiety and panic throughout my day. This wasn't something that reading a Bible verse a day was able to fix either. This issue took experiencing God's patience with me and his grace toward me, each and every day. I practiced approaching God after I messed up, confessing and repenting, and watching how he didn't spend the next week "not talking to me because he was mad at me," or "lecturing me," or "beating me down with his word." Instead, God received me into his loving arms and reminded me of who I was in him. I used to be so scared of approaching him when I messed up; now I run to him, and cry, and confess, because I know that he is the best Comforter there will ever be. Try it for yourself and see how restored you'll feel after having a heart-to-heart with the Redeemer of your soul! David said it best in Ps 23:3: "He refreshes my soul. He guides me along the right paths for his name's sake."

A Question to Ponder

If God were to describe me in three adjectives, which adjectives would he use?

____

____

____

God Keeps No Record of Wrongs

In child therapy, one of the strategies mental health professionals use is called a *behavior thermometer*. The thermometer is sectioned into different colors or gradients, representing how well or how badly you're behaving. Take a look below:

A. I'm safe with God.
B. I'm one mistake away from God giving up on me.
C. God is angry with me and has abandoned me.

In my early years as a believer, I believed that although I may have confessed my sins, God was still keeping score. I walked around believing that every sin I committed was piled up in some heavenly chart, and that I was alternating between B and C with God. This fear led me to question how truly secure I was in God's love. I feared that one day he was going to throw in the towel and say, "I'm done, you're just too much. You can go and become someone else's problem!" This mindset led me to strive for other ways to meet my sense of security. I'll go over some of the ways we tend to use in the chapters that follow. The thought process I was stuck in caused me to walk around plagued with fear that I'd need to figure out a fallback in case God "threw me out." It's a scary place to be in. It's a scary thought to live with day in and day out. If this section resonates with you, please hear me out; we all make mistakes. In 1

John 1:9, God promises, "If we confess our sins, he is faithful and just and will forgive us our sins and purify us from all unrighteousness." When it comes to the extent of God's forgiveness, David describes it like this: "As far as the east is from the west, so far has he removed our transgressions from us" (Ps 103:12).

My prayer for you when you mess up is this: may you run toward your heavenly Father and confess to him. And may you be reminded that in Jesus, his forgiveness is from beginning to end.

A Question to Ponder

When I approach God, do I view him as a Judge who's ready to lecture me or as my heavenly Father who's ready to receive me with open arms?

____

____

____

God Does Not Delight in Evil but Rejoices with the Truth

One of the most popular Bible passages is Ps 139. The psalm starts out with David praising God for the way he made him. The psalm gives God glory for his presence in our lives. David closes the psalm with this: "Search me, God, and know my heart; test me and know my anxious thoughts. See if there is any offensive way in me, and lead me in the way everlasting" (Ps 139:23–24). I used to read this psalm and stop before this verse. To be honest, I wasn't comfortable asking God to show me how I was offending him, because I felt that I was plenty aware of my list of offenses; and I wasn't fond of the idea of reminding God of how much I'd offended him, because what if looking at how badly I'd messed up made God change his mind about me? Do you ever think like that? In counseling my patients, I discovered that plenty of them thought like I once did. The enemy had deceived me and he had deceived them;

no wonder why the number one diagnosed mental health disorder according to the World Health Organization (WHO) is generalized anxiety disorder!

It wasn't until one day, as I was reading Ps 139 that verses 23 and 24 jumped out at me. David wasn't asking God to remind him of how sinful he was. David was asking God to point out to him any faulty thoughts he held about God that ultimately kept David from becoming all that God created him to be. God wants to heal you. As you walk with him, he wants you to seek him and ask him to heal any erroneous thinking you currently hold so that you can be all that he created you to be. Ask him! He is faithful to show you.

A Question to Ponder

What negative beliefs do I currently have about God?

____

____

____

God Always Protects

You can read one encounter after another in the Bible about God's protective nature. I've been fortunate to have experienced God's protection throughout my life. Leaving Islam resulted in persecution by my family of origin. Over the course of nine years, my relatives made several attempts to come after my family and I, yet with every attempt, I watched how God protected my husband, my kids, and me. With every attempt, my faith grew. I remember the first time my relatives showed up to confront me about my conversion to Christianity. I had been a believer for only a few years at the time, so my trust in God's protective love for me was still on shaky ground. As my relatives banged on doors and attempted to open windows in our home, my husband and I crawled on the floor and waited for the police to show up. Fast-forward to seven years, two kids, and several persecution attempts later, my faith in

God is unshakable. In fact, the last time we were confronted, with God's help, I was able to stand my ground and ask them to leave. I know that nothing can ever happen to me outside of God's will, and since I rest on his unconditional love for me, I know that his will is my best option. I'm not just saying that because it sounds good. I'm saying it because through the years of walking with God and witnessing how protective he is, I am convinced that I have found what I've been craving all my life—A secure and an unshakable shelter. The cool thing is he offers the same for you. God wants to father you, not to lecture you but to protect you and guide you; most of all, he wants to lavish his love on you. You just have to receive it.

A Question to Ponder

What has God protected me from in the last five years?

____

____

____

God Always Trusts

When I refer to trust, I don't mean that God *blindly* trusts. I'm referring to the fact that God knows everything about you. He knows you more than you could ever know yourself. He knows the good, the bad, and the ugly, yet he *chooses* to love you. God's choice to love you is unconditional, not based on your performance but based on his nature. As we uncovered earlier in this section, God is love; and God wants us as his children to demonstrate his love to others. To drive this point home, Jesus told his disciples: "You have heard that it was said, 'Love your neighbor and hate your enemy.' But I tell you, love your enemies and pray for those who persecute you, that you may be children of your Father in heaven. He causes his sun to rise on the evil and the good, and sends rain on the righteous and the unrighteous. If you love those who love you, what reward will you get? Are not even the tax collectors doing that?" (Matt 5:43–46).

In other words, just as God loved us when we were unlovable, and he continues to stick with us through thick and thin, we are to love those who are hard to love. I know it's much easier said than done, but remember, if he's telling you to do it, then he will equip you to carry it out. I'd like to encourage you to ask God to show you what loving someone the right way looks like in your life. It can mean that you no longer enable your loved one who's been stuck in addiction, but instead, tell them they must go to rehab. It may be inviting your neighbor over for Thanksgiving dinner. It may be sending an encouraging text to a friend who is struggling with fertility treatments. Ask God, and he will be faithful to show you.

A Question to Ponder

In what area of my life do I need to see God's power at hand?

____

____

____

God Always Hopes

The word "hope" comes from the Greek word *elpidzo*, meaning "to hope or wait with full confidence." (If you're interested in this and more definitions of Greek words, a simple place to look them up is on Bible Hub—see www.biblehub.com.)

The Bible tells a story of a king named Jehoshaphat. In the beginning of Jehoshaphat's reign, Jehoshaphat consulted only the Lord, and the Bible says that the Lord was with him. A little while later, King Jehoshaphat made a mistake by entering into a partnership with one of the worst kings ever recorded in the history of the Bible—King Ahab, husband to Jezebel. God wasn't in the midst of this partnership, and the king certainly didn't seek the counsel of the Lord before entering into this partnership. Throughout the course of their alliance, King Jehoshaphat and King Ahab decided to go to war against a city. As the battle was raging, King Jehoshaphat saw that he was about to be overtaken. In desperation, he cried out to the Lord. The Bible says: "Jehoshaphat cried out, and the Lord helped him. God drew them away from him (2 Chron 18:31b). When he got to the palace safely, a messenger from the Lord went to King Jehoshaphat and confronted him about the decision that he made to partner with a terrible king, yet closed the meeting with "there is, however, some good in you, for you have rid the land of the Asherah poles and have set your heart on seeking God" (2 Chron 19:3). In other words, God was saying, "Although you made a bad decision, I still believe in you." How many of us need to hear this today?

People often shy away from seeking God out of fear he won't accept them due to past mistakes. When counseling my patients, I would often hear: "You don't know everything that I've done in the past." My response would often be: "I don't, but regardless of what you've done, there is nothing that you could have ever done or could ever do that outweighs Jesus's sacrifice on your behalf." When Jesus said, "It is finished" (see John 19:30), he meant that once you surrender your life to him, your sins from beginning until you take your last breath are erased. Just as Col 1:21–22 says: "Once you were alienated from God and were enemies in your minds because of your evil behavior. But now he has reconciled you by Christ's physical body through death to present you holy in his sight, without blemish and free from accusation." Out of his unconditional love for us, we have hope! Because of what Jesus did for you and me, we have full access to God as our Father. When we approach him, he receives us as his beloved children, and when we mess up, we can cry out to him. He is the Father who pulls us out of the trenches, the One who cleans us up and says: "You may have messed up but you are not a mess-up. I believe in you, let's try again tomorrow."

A Question to Ponder

With which negative behaviors do I struggle, that I need to surrender to God?

____

____

____

God Always Perseveres

How many of us experience fear and anxiety when we mess up because we think, "That's it, I blew it with God, he's done with me!" As
you can tell from the bits and pieces of my story that I've shared with
you, I've lived many years believing this. Even as a therapist, I can
attest that this thought process dominated my patients too!

The truth of the matter is, God's love toward you is not con-
ditional. When you decided to surrender your life to Jesus, God
adopted you as his and marked you as his child by putting his Holy
Spirit in you. The Bible says it like this: "And when you believed in
Christ, he identified you as his own by giving you the Holy Spirit,
whom he promised long ago. The Spirit is God's guarantee that he
will give us the inheritance he promised and that he has purchased
us to be his own people" (Eph 1:13b–14a NLT). So from that time
forward, God's Holy Spirit guides you, helps you, comforts you,
consoles you; and when you mess up, God's Spirit convicts you for
the purpose of restoring you to the person you truly are in him.
God offers you an enduring love that outlasts this life. In times
when you find yourself fearful of God and dread approaching him,
just remember what Paul said in Rom 8:15–16: "So you have not
received a spirit that makes you fearful slaves. Instead, you received
God's Spirit when he adopted you as his own children. Now we call
him, 'Abba, Father.' For his Spirit joins with our spirit to affirm
that we are God's children" (NLT). God's love for you perseveres
through your good days and your bad days. In Jesus, God's love for
you is irrevocable.

The enemy knows this; that's why day and night he works hard to convince you that your status before God is contingent on your behavior. That is sheer legalism. Jesus fulfilled the requirements of the law because we couldn't. Does this mean we'll never sin again? Absolutely not! Our sinful nature is still at war within us even as we walk with God. However, the closer we walk with God and the more we learn to lean on God, the less power we will give our sinful nature. God's persevering love toward us is a promise that he will carry us through thick and thin. In Jesus, your heavenly Father made a pledge to you to preserve your soul until he calls you to eternal life with him. God's attribute of perseverance gives you hope that "he [God] who began a good work in you will carry it on to completion until the day of Christ Jesus" (Phil 1:6). What's your responsibility in this matter? Continue to seek him. Even after you feel like you've failed him, go back to him and seek his face. He won't strike you down. He won't push you away. He won't shame you. Instead, his persevering love will welcome you with open arms. Jesus knew we would encounter periods in our lives when we fail to recognize our identity in Christ and strive to draw our sense of self from the world. When we fall into temptation, we must repent, and turn back to God. Jesus showed us how God would respond to our repentance in the parable of the prodigal son. If you're not familiar with the story, please read it in Luke 15:11–32. The passage tells of a father who had two sons. The youngest decided to take his share of his inheritance before his father's death, went off, and squandered it on a reckless living. After he spent all he had, he got a job to make ends meet, but the working conditions were bad. One day, the prodigal son came to his senses and decided to humble himself, go back to his father, and ask his father to hire him as one of his servants, so that he could at least eat better than his current working conditions allowed for. Here is how the story ends:

> And he arose and came to his father. But while he was still a long way off, his father saw him and felt compassion, and ran and embraced him and kissed him. And the son said to him, "Father, I have sinned against heaven and before you. I am no longer worthy to be called your

son." But the father said to his servants,"Bring quickly the best robe, and put it on him, and put a ring on his hand, and shoes on his feet. And bring the fattened calf and kill it, and let us eat and celebrate. For this my son was dead, and is alive again; he was lost, and is found." And they began to celebrate. (Luke 15:20–24)

Any time you're tempted to flee from God, remember that his love for you perseveres past your mistakes. There is nothing that you have done in the past that would obliterate God's love for you in Jesus. Turn back to him. He's waiting on you with open arms. He is committed to seeing you through.

A Question to Ponder

In what area in my life do I need assurance of God's persevering love for me?

____

____

____

God Never Fails

This attribute speaks to God's faithfulness. We often attribute our relationship with God to our "holding on" to God, when in reality, it is his grace that sustains us every single day. We will never know how many heartaches God has protected us from on this side of heaven. His faithfulness is what carries us through life's trials and difficulties. His promise is to be here with us every step of the way. To never leave us or forsake us. To surround us with his shield. To strengthen us physically, emotionally, and spiritually. To comfort us when we are sad. To counsel us and guide us when we need wisdom; and if we let him, he will be our closest companion in this life's journey.

A Question to Ponder

When in my life do I need to practice seeking God more (i.e., when I need comfort, when I need wisdom, etc.)?

____
____

____

CHAPTER 6

Developing a Secure Relationship with God

IN MY EARLY YEARS of walking with God, I hesitated approaching him because I imagined God taking out a scroll and listing everything I had done wrong since my last visit with him. As we discussed in the last chapter, this is not how God is. The fact of the matter is, when you surrendered your life to Jesus, you became a son or a daughter of a loving, sovereign God. If you have not surrendered your life to Jesus and would like to do so, please pray the following prayer: "God, I know that I am a sinner in need of a Savior, and that Savior is Jesus Christ. I believe that out of your love for me you sent Jesus to die on the cross for my sins. Please forgive my sins and be my Lord and Savior." If you prayed the above prayer, welcome to the family!

After I gave my life to Jesus, I spent years afraid that any time I approached God, it would turn into a lecture from him. I spent years praying, then cringing as I waited for God to tell me what I did wrong. As children of God, we're told: "Let us then approach God's throne of grace with confidence, so that we may receive mercy and find grace to help us in our time of need" (Heb 4:16).

My first couple of years as a child of God I more so tiptoed around the throne of grace, rather than approaching the throne of grace with confidence, because of my old patterns of thinking.

To be honest with you, this process is not an overnight process. This isn't a magic formula that'll get you from point A to point B in a split second, especially if you grew up in an oppressive or an abusive environment where your sense of safety was nonexistent.

This process takes developing a relationship from the ground up—which means you will have times when you mess up and spend the next three days waiting on God to strike you down, only to find out, that's not how God operates.

I walked through many days in my life living in the following pattern: I messed up, hid from God because of shame, then came out of hiding, and did well for a little while. Then got right back at it again.

The problems with thinking we can hide from God after messing up is it's unbiblical, and it doesn't help us at all. See Ps 139:7–12:

> Where can I go from your Spirit? Where can I flee from your presence? If I go up to the heavens, you are there; if I make my bed in the depths, you are there. If I rise on the wings of the dawn, if I settle on the far side of the sea, even there your hand will guide me, your right hand will hold me fast. If I say, "Surely the darkness will hide me and the light become night around me," even the darkness will not be dark to you; the night will shine like the day, for darkness is as light to you.

This passage used to scare me, because it opened my eyes to the reality that God is ever-present. Nothing is ever hidden from him. However, as I got to know God, this passage brought me comfort in knowing that his eyes were always on me, which is what I craved but was scared of at the same time.

A Question to Ponder

How does the fact that *nothing that you do* is hidden from God make you feel? (Be honest!)

____

____

____

As I drew close to God, when I sinned, I started to not feel okay with covering up my sin. In 1 John 1:8–9, God's word says: "If we claim to be without sin, we deceive ourselves and the truth is not in us. If we confess our sins, he is faithful and just and will forgive us our sins and purify us from all unrighteousness."

Describe a time when you messed up and your mistake didn't sit well with you until you confessed it to someone:

____

____

____

It was in the process of coming to God and saying, "I'm sorry I messed up," truly feeling the brokenness of my "self-striving," and repenting, then feeling his grace and mercy towards me, that I started seeing God as 1 Cor 13:4–7 describes him, as we went over in the previous chapter.

Punishment vs. Discipline

Most highways have rumble strips on the side of the road, designed to keep you from running off course. If you drift off your lane, as your tires land on the strips, your car will make a startling noise to get your attention. God's discipline works in a similar fashion. Before Jesus left, he told his disciples that he would not leave them as orphans. In other words, he reassured them that he didn't show up and walk with them, just to leave them unguided. Jesus told his disciples that the Holy Spirit would come and guide them throughout their mission here on earth until he came back to get them. The Holy Spirit will not only guide you and counsel you; he will also act as a rumble strip when you start drifting off course.

God loves you too much to allow you to drift off without getting your attention. One of the markers of a healthy relationship is accountability. Living as a child of God means that God loves you enough to tell you when you're getting off course. Take a look at Heb 12:5–7: "And have you completely forgotten this word of encouragement that addresses you as a father addresses his son? It says, 'My son, do not make light of the Lord's discipline, and do not lose heart when he rebukes you, because the Lord disciplines the one he loves, and he chastens everyone he accepts as his son.' Endure hardship as discipline; God is treating you as his children. For what children are not disciplined by their father?"

If you were raised in an environment where discipline meant punishment, you may find the word "discipline" triggering. Let me clarify what the true definition of discipline is: correction for the purpose of restoration. I have two kids. When they misbehave, it's my responsibility as their parent to correct them. When God corrects you, it is for the purpose of restoring you to the person you are in Christ. As God's child, God will never, ever shame you— meaning, if you feel that God is saying, "Shame on you," "You're a loser," "You're a mistake," etc., that's not the voice of God. His voice is more like "You're better than that," "That wasn't the right decision," "Go apologize and make it right." God's purpose for discipline is to restore you back to your true identity in Christ.

The Bible is filled with stories of people who were disciplined by God. Take Jonah's life, for example. As we discussed earlier, he was aware of God's goodness, but he showed contempt for God's sovereignty. God chose Jonah to deliver a message of repentance to the people of Nineveh. Jonah didn't agree that "those people" deserved to be saved from God's wrath, which reflected pride on Jonah's part. What happened next? God disciplined Jonah by reminding him of his sovereignty over all of his creation. Jonah humbled himself and repented, and God forgave him. The next time God disciplines you, I'd like to encourage you to heed God's leading and to thank him for his presence in your life. If you're tempted to hide from God in fear, remember, God is not shaming you. God's not ashamed of you. God is committed to you. He loves you. His purpose of disciplining you is to remind you "Hey, that's not who you are."

Describe a time when God disciplined you and your response (fear):

____

____

____

Describe a time when God disciplined you and your response (assurance):

____

____

____

CHAPTER 7

Living as a Secure Child of God

REMEMBER, AS A BELIEVER in Jesus, God allows you to "approach the throne of grace confidently," as it says in Heb 4:16. Knowing this verse and actually living it out are two totally different things! As I had mentioned before, it took me years to actually approach God confidently. The first handful of times I approached God about a hurt, I was waiting for God's response to be: "Okay, first-world problem, get to the back of the line." But it wasn't! God wants us to approach him with our worries and our hurts because he is the only one who can heal them completely. I know it's easier for me to say this to you now, but I'm sharing parts of my story with you because I don't want you to make the same mistake I made, by spending too much time tiptoeing around the throne of grace, rather than approaching the throne of grace confidently as it says for us to do in Heb 4:16. So, I'd like to encourage you to do the following exercise I've given my patients:

Commit to spending your first part of the morning with God for seven days. Dedicate twenty minutes. No phone. No distractions. Get a devotional, or read a passage of the Bible and ask God to show you how this passage applies to you. God is faithful. He shows up. Ask God to help you recognize his promptings. Ask God to show you in tangible ways that he is with you. Try spending time with him for seven days, and before you know it, you won't exchange time with him for anything!

View God as He Truly Is

Earlier in the book, we went over a list of God's characteristics. It is so important to become familiar with these characteristics because this is where the enemy tends to target God's children the most. Remember, what led to the fall began with Eve questioning God's character. The enemy wants you to question God's character. If he can get you to doubt who God says he is, you'll start drifting away from your destiny. Whenever you feel anxiety creeping in or start feeling like God is not with you or that God is not for you, I want to encourage you to use a helpful technique that I have used in my life and I have invited my patients to use in theirs. Go back to the characteristics of God that we explored together earlier. Out of the list, pick two characteristics that would be most helpful to combat your *current* thought process, and meditate on those characteristics throughout the day for twenty-one days. Take a look at the chart below as a guide:

The Truth	The Enemy's Lie	God's Truth
God is patient.	God is fed up with me.	In Jesus, God shows me just how merciful he is toward me. God's mercy for me is new each and every day (see Lam 3:22–23).
God is kind.	God is mad at me.	In Jesus, God has shown me his kindness. He sees through my sins, yet he still pursues me because he wants to heal my brokenness that led to my sin pattern (see Luke 4:18).

God does not envy.	God wants to take away good things from me.	Every good and perfect gift came from God (see Jas 1:17).
God does not boast.	God is distant from me.	In Jesus, God opened the way for me to have a relationship with him (see John 14:6).
God is not proud.	God scoffs at me.	In Jesus, God showed me the extent of his love for me (see Rom 8:32).
God does not dishonor others.	God is ashamed of me.	In Jesus, God exchanged my shame for his honor (see 2 Cor 5:21).
God is not self-seeking.	God just wants to control me.	In Jesus, God gave up his own Son for me to be in a relationship with him (see Rom 8:32).
God is not easily angered.	God is punishing me.	In Jesus, God exchanged his rightful anger toward me for his mercy for once and for all (see Rom 5:8).
God keeps no record of wrongs.	God still holds my sin over my head.	In Jesus, God forgives my sins of yesterday, today, and for eternity (see 1 John 1:9).
God does not delight in evil.	God caused bad things to happen to me because he was holding my sin against me.	In Jesus, God punished evil so that he can extend his mercy to me (see Eph 2:4–5).
God rejoices with the truth.	God doesn't care if I sin or if I don't.	When I act in a way that is incongruent with my identity in Christ, God will by his Holy Spirit convict me in order to restore me (see Heb 12:5–7).

God always protects.	God is against me.	In Jesus, God shows me that he is for me (see Rom 8:31).
God always trusts.	God has had enough with me.	In Jesus, nothing can separate me from the love of God (see Rom 8:38–39).
God always hopes.	I'm too far gone for God.	Jesus is actively interceding for me (see Heb 7:25).
God always perseveres.	God has given up on me.	In Jesus, God was showing me that he is committed to seeing me through (see Phil 1:6).
God never fails.	God invested in the wrong person. I keep failing him.	In Jesus, God has put his Holy Spirit in me as a seal marking me as his. God has secured a place for me for eternity (see Eph 1:13–14).

View Yourself as You Truly Are

God is the safest Father you could ever have. He literally breathed life into your lungs. He controls every beat of your heart. He created you to bear his image because he loves you. He was looking out for your safety from before you were even born. He has your best interest at heart. There will never be anyone in this whole world who looks out for you as much as he does. Even when you mess up, the Bible says: "But God demonstrates his own love for us in this: While we were still sinners, Christ died for us" (Rom 5:8).

Devote Yourself to Him

Our lack of devotion to God often stems from lack of understanding of God's character and attributes. The Bible says: "My people are being destroyed because they don't know me" (Hos 4:6a NLT).

Our sense of safety is filled perfectly when we rely on God's sovereignty and his goodness to fill it. Again, 1) God is the most powerful Person ever. 2) God is committed to your best interest. As I said before, devote the first part of your day to him. When you see for yourself that he shows up, you will get into the habit of including him in your day-to-day decisions!

Distinguish Warning from Threat

Throughout Scripture, God warns us of the consequences of not being fully devoted to him. God's nature is to protect us against our own self-destructive behaviors; therefore, God issues warnings for our protection. Nobody likes warnings. I mean, I've never heard someone say, "Thank God my 'check engine' light came on!" However, in hindsight, we're glad we received the warning so that we could make the necessary adjustments before the issue got worse. God is the most powerful Person ever. He created everything that has ever existed, including you. He created you for a purpose. He wants you to achieve your purpose, so when you go off track, he is committed enough to you to remind you and help you get back on track. You have to seek him and get familiar with his voice. God will never threaten you. Threats are used to induce fear. Threats come from the enemy, and their intent is to paralyze you with fear. Warnings come from God, and their intent is to restore you to your true purpose.

Approach God When You've Messed Up

There have been times when I've messed up and I've needed to repent. Well, the first couple of times of approaching God when I messed up, I was waiting for lightning to fall down on me. It didn't. God's word says: "If we confess our sins, he is faithful and just and will forgive us our sins and purify us from all unrighteousness" (1 John 1:9).

Now, this isn't a license to sin and confess. The Bible warns about taking the grace we've been given for granted. Take a look at Rom 6:1–2: "What shall we say, then? Shall we go on sinning so that grace may increase? By no means! We are those who have died to sin; how can we live in it any longer?" In Rom 6:11–14, Paul continues, "In the same way, count yourselves dead to sin but alive to God in Christ Jesus. Therefore do not let sin reign in your mortal body so that you obey its evil desires. Do not offer any part of yourself to sin as an instrument of wickedness, but rather offer yourselves to God as those who have been brought from death to life; and offer every part of yourself to him as an instrument of righteousness. For sin shall no longer be your master, because you are not under the law, but under grace."

Does this mean that we are not going to mess up? No, we are. Look at this! The same Paul who wrote Rom 6 was transparent about his war with his sinful nature as a child of God: "For in my inner being I delight in God's law; but I see another law at work in me, waging war against the law of my mind and making me a prisoner of the law of sin at work within me. What a wretched man I am! Who will rescue me from this body that is subject to death? Thanks be to God, who delivers me through Jesus Christ our Lord!" (Rom 7:22–25a).

Therefore, when you mess up, and when I mess up, instead of running from God, let's commit to running to our heavenly Father, who loves us and is ready to help us. Follow the following steps: confess, repent, and receive God's forgiveness.

CHAPTER 8

Healing My Insecurity Wounds

THE FOLLOWING PAGES CONTAIN exercises and prayers I've used with patients to help them draw closer to God and break ties with dead ends. Take a look.

Self-Reliance

If self-reliance is an area you tend to run to in order to find security, please use the following template:

1. **Confess** to God that you are stuck in this trap by praying something like this: "Father, I confess that I've been relying on myself. Father, thank you for showing me this. Father, please forgive me and help me to rely on you alone."

2. **Ask** God to reveal the root of your self-reliance by praying the following prayer: "Faithful Father, thank you for leading me this far. Father, I ask that you'll reveal where my self-reliance is rooted. Father, as you reveal memories, I ask for your grace, in Jesus's name. Amen."

3. **Examine** where your self-reliance began:

____

____

____

4. **Uncover** and write down the lies you've been believing about yourself as a result of the experience(s). These lies often began with the pronoun I—(e.g., "I am not good enough").

____

____

____

5. **Forgive**. Forgiveness is the key that unlocks the chains you are bound to. There is no way around it. "Father, show me who I need to forgive, where I need your healing. Father, shine your truth on my life."

Name:____

Offense:____

How their behavior affected you:____

As a result of this, I feel [angry, sad, unworthy, ashamed, afraid, alone, stupid, etc.].

When God shows you, follow through with "God, I choose to forgive [name] for [offense]. [Name]'s actions made me feel [feeling]."

6. **Trust** in the healing that God has done in your life and thank him. "Father, thank you for healing me. Father, thank you for your ever-present Spirit who is with me. Please set your hedge of protection over me and continue to lead me in Jesus's name."

The prayers and steps I included in this portion can be applied to the "money" and to the "people-pleasing" sections. For the sake of simplicity, they're included in only one section.

People-Pleasing

The way I've helped my patients to transition from relying on others to relying on God as their primary source of security is by assigning my patients homework, in which they practiced seeking God for one decision a week, then the next month, two to three decisions per week. As they grew comfortable seeking God's wisdom, the chains of bondage they had with their God-substitute unlinked one after another.

A word of caution: when applying this method yourself or with someone else, please know that there will be times when the person you used to seek security from—whether it's a friend, parent, mentor—will get upset with you for not asking their advice as much. This is an indication that the person you sought safety from was getting their need for significance (a need we will uncover in the next chapters) met by you. It is not your job or your responsibility to meet this need for the person. It is not your job to make the person feel better. Repeat after me: "I do not owe this person an explanation. I am free to live in the freedom God called me to live in." Pray for them, from a distance if you have to. And please, do not go back to your old ways.

If you've reached this step and you find yourself in a situation where you're cut off from your only source of support, you're going to be tempted to go back to your old ways because you feel that unhealthy support is better than no support at all. That's a trap. Do *not* do it.

Your next step is to find a counselor. There's no shame in counseling. Please don't go from seeking one unhealthy source to seeking another. Please don't call Dad to gossip about Mom who stopped talking to you for not asking her for advice. That only breeds drama. A counselor will be an unbiased person who will listen to you, affirm you, challenge you, encourage you when you need it, and hold you accountable to live out the calling that God has on your life. A counselor can either serve as a mentor or help you discern a healthy mentor in your life.

Indicators of a healthy mentor include:

A. **Presence:** They make time for you (preferably weekly).

B. **Encouragement:** They continually encourage you to grow in your relationship with God.

C. **Accountability:** They hold you accountable when you stray, or when you make decisions that are not congruent with who you are in Christ.

D. **Applause:** They applaud the steps you're taking to grow in Christ.

E. **Leading:** They lead you toward God, not toward themselves.

Remember

The goal of having a healthy mentor is to help you grow in a relationship with God, not with the mentor. Regardless of how great your mentor's life may seem, no one will ever be a good enough substitute for God.

The following is an example of a healthy exchange with a mentor:

You have an issue; you're in the habit of calling the mentor first. The mentor answers the phone, listens, and affirms. Then the mentor models how to seek God's wisdom to process through the problem. The mentor will pray with you and hang up the phone. The mentor will pray for you as you seek God first. As you grow in your relationship with God, you'll call your mentor with solutions that you believe God has provided you with. Over time, your need for your mentor will decrease, and your trust in God's love for you will increase and fill that void.

There are people who are supposed to be in your life only for a season. If you place your sense of safety in people, you'll find yourself trying to hold on and make a relationship that was intended only for a season last a lifetime. Letting go of someone whose purpose in your life has ended is painful. But it will be even more painful if that person filled the need for security for you throughout the course of your relationship. This was often the case when I treated patients who struggled with grief.

Grief is a painful journey in life that none of us opts to go through. Losing someone you love is awful. The days of grieving seem long and endless. There are times when we think we're ready because the person we lost suffered from long dreadful years of terminal illness, only to find ourselves crumbled when our loved one takes his or her last breath. There are times when the loss catches us by surprise, such as in situations where a car accident claims our loved one's life. The loss seems so sudden that we find ourselves replaying the last time we saw our loved one over and over again.

Grieving the loss of a loved one is a necessary and healthy process. There are no timelines for grief. Gaining closure from the loss you experienced doesn't indicate that your grief was any less painful, and it certainly doesn't indicate that you've "moved on." Accepting the loss you experienced is a choice that you make. It shows that you have decided to move forward.

There are times when your grief symptoms don't seem to get better over the years. Times when you feel like "it's been years, and it still feels like it was just yesterday that it happened, and I just can't move past losing him/her." Times when you feel like you've lost your sense of joy and your sense of purpose in life. The above are indicators that your grief has become "complicated grief."

Take a look at the difference below:

Grief Symptoms	Complicated Grief Symptoms
Crying, sobbing, feelings of anger	Strong yearning for the person you lost that seems to get worse over time
Sleep problems	Distress when reminded of the person you lost
Lack of energy	Inability to accept the loss of a loved one
Difficulty concentrating	Inability to focus on anything but the loss

As I mentioned before, there is no timeline to grief. However, symptoms differ between the two types of grief. People who experience complicated grief often say that they feel "trapped" or "stuck" in their grief. In my experience, both personally and clinically, we are most likely to experience complicated grief if the person we lost was our source of safety, comfort, and security. So many patients sat on my couch crying without consolation because they felt like they lost the one person who cared for them most. The one person they could call on when needed. The one person who served as their anchor. If this is where you are, I am so sorry. I wish I could take your pain away. I'm often asked, "Where do I go from here?"

I know that when you're in the midst of grief, the last thing you want to hear is a Bible verse. This is especially true if you feel that God took your loved one from you or you feel that God didn't help you resolve your marital problems that ended in divorce. Whatever pain you are feeling right now, I want to invite you to take a moment and cry out to God. "Why should I?" you might ask. "He didn't listen to me when I begged and pleaded with him to heal [name of loved one] from [illness]" or "Where was God when I wanted my marriage restored?" The truth is: he was right there with you.

There is a well-known poem called "Footprints" by Mary Stevenson. This poem is a fictional dialogue between Jesus and a person who has endured a series of hardships. By the end of the person's plea to Jesus, he/she finds out that God was there all along.

This poem is a great reminder of God's faithfulness through life's hardships. If you've never read it, I encourage you to!

My point is, God was in the midst of your pain. I don't know why your prayer wasn't answered, but I can promise you this, it is not because God doesn't care for you. So if you're mad at him, he already knows. I want to invite you to tell him. Cry out to him. Seek him. Exposing your heart to God will not make him love you any less. That's what the psalmists did. Take a look:

- My soul is in deep anguish. How long, LORD, how long? (Ps 6:3)

- All my longings lie open before you, LORD; my sighing is not hidden from you. My heart pounds, my strength fails me; even the light has gone from my eyes. My friends and companions avoid me because of my wounds; my neighbors stay far away. (Ps 38:9–11)

- I weep with sorrow; encourage me by your word. (Ps 119: 28 NLT)

I could go on and on, listing one psalm account after another where a psalmist expressed grief, sorrow, anguish, anger, and despair to God. Not one of them got struck down by God for seeking relief. You may never know why your prayer wasn't answered, but what you will receive in seeking God is his presence. And where his presence is, there is joy, peace, and comfort.

If this is where you find yourself, I pray the following prayer over you:

> Faithful Father, I lift this brother or sister in Christ up to you right now. Father, I don't know exactly what they are going through. I don't know the details of their grief, but, Lord, you do. Father, right now, as they are seeking you, I pray that they will feel your presence ever so tangibly. Father, I pray that you will shield them with your peace. Father, I pray that they will feel your comfort like never before. I pray that you will put a hedge of protection over their mind, over their soul, over their heart, and I pray that depression and anxiety will flee from them. I pray

that as they go about the coming days, weeks, months, and years, that you will draw them close to you—that they'll come to grasp your tangible love for them and that they'll know with full assurance that you love them more than anyone could ever love them. In Jesus's name. Amen.

Acceptance

For you did not receive the spirit of bondage again to fear, but you received the Spirit of adoption by whom we cry out, "Abba, Father."

—ROM 8:15 NKJV

CHAPTER 9

My Need for Acceptance

IN THIS SECTION I will use the terms "belonging" and "acceptance" interchangeably to discuss this need. Just as a feeling of security calms our nervous system and reduces our level of anxiety, feeling like we are accepted increases a chemical in our brains called serotonin, which combats depression and makes us feel happy. Our need to belong with others dates back to the creation of Adam. A little while after creating Adam, "the LORD God said, 'It is not good for the man to be alone. I will make a helper suitable for him'" (Gen 2:18). Your need for a relationship with other human beings was something that God saw as beneficial for you, in addition to your relationship with him.

The difference between our relationship with God and our relationship with others is in the level of dependence we are wired for. We were created to be dependent on God and interdependent with other people.

Dependence on God

This means you rely on him as your Source for your needs.

Interdependence with People

This means you rely on one another to sharpen, strengthen, and encourage one another to become more like Jesus.

In my years as a counselor, I found that we often fall into depression, anxiety, or both when we switch the two—meaning we live "dependent on people" yet "interdependent with God." That is dangerous territory right there. Here is what it looks like:

Interdependence with God

This means that you check in with God when you need something. You tend to pray when you have a need. God is not invited into every area of your life, because you hold a view of him that makes him seem unsafe. So you set boundaries with God and you keep him at arm's length.

Dependence on People

This means you have a person or a few individuals that you rely on for areas of your life. You feel anxious or depressed when you haven't received attention from these individuals, so you strive for it. You feel needy at times, or you have been referred to as needy by people.

Again, switching who we are dependent upon and who we are to be interdependent with is a common issue that we will discuss throughout the next few pages.

CHAPTER 10

My Striving for Acceptance

I HAVE TREATED MANY patients and have overseen cases where patients carried with them deep wounds from childhood that resulted in them feeling like they were not good enough to belong to their families or to be accepted by their loved ones. I've also seen where patients had great childhoods, yet still felt like something was missing resulting in them feeling like they didn't belong. Whichever end of the spectrum you fall into, as long as we live on this side of eternity, we are going to encounter issues; and if we are not secure in our relationship with God, our human nature will pull us to fulfill our need for acceptance and belonging from what we've been referring to in this book as dead ends.

Throughout the following pages, we are going to identify these dead ends and explore how we use each one of them to attain a false sense of belonging. In my history of counseling and reviewing case files with our counselors, I have identified the following three most used dead ends: works, being needed, and people-pleasing.

Here is a prayer before we begin: "Heavenly Father, you are the ultimate provider. Father, I confess that there have been times when I sought acceptance from sources outside of you. As I go through the next few sections, please show me where I am currently seeking to fulfill my sense of belonging independent of you, and help me to meet this need in you. Amen."

Striving through Works to Earn Favor with God

If we had been able to achieve our way to being good enough for God to accept us, he wouldn't have given his only Son for us. The Bible is clear in Isa 64:6: "All our righteous acts are like filthy rags." This means that in comparison to God's holiness, even our best behavior doesn't come close to measuring up to his standard to accept us. On our own, we were helpless to ever achieve the status of holiness required for God to accept us as his own. Thankfully, God knew where we stood in comparison to his standards; he sent Jesus to do what we couldn't do. So if you surrendered your life to Jesus, your new status became son/daughter of God.

Another way we can fall into this dead end is when we believe that we need to continue to prove to God that we are worthy to be his children. This thought process usually stems from lack of security in our relationships growing up. Perhaps you had a parent who wasn't happy with you unless you made straight A's. Or parents who expected too much out of you, and when you fell short, they let you know how disappointed they were. Going through experiences similar to these makes the grace of God sound too good to be true. Even when we accept his grace by faith, until our experiences of rejection are healed, we fall into the habit of working hard to make sure God doesn't reject us the way our parent(s) did. I fell into this trap for many years. I volunteered at church out of obligation to God for all that he saved me from. I felt like I needed to show my gratitude through ministry-related community service as a way of showing God that I was serious about living for him. Throughout the years, as I walked this life journey with many people, I realized that this trap was a common one. In fact, this mindset was so prevalent during the apostle Paul's lifetime, Paul addressed it in one of his letters to the church of Galatia. Let's take a look at what the apostle Paul said in Gal 3:3: "Are you so foolish?

After beginning by means of the Spirit, are you now trying to finish by means of the flesh?" Paul was clear that no human effort can ever come close to satisfying God's standard. Our only hope is Christ. We are to cling to him alone. Christ's ability to sustain us in this life is like an airplane that has the capacity to fly. Christ is the airplane, and you and I are the passengers. We cannot fly on our own because we're not wired that way. Therefore, our trying to maintain what only Christ has the capacity to attain and maintain for us is like us going on an airplane and deciding to jump off midway and fly on our own. We can certainly jump off, but it'll be to our detriment. That's what our self-striving attempts do to us.

The apostle Paul's point is still relevant today. Jesus freed us from the burden of the law. Our works must never be a means to attain or to maintain his love, but a means to convey it to those he is calling to himself.

A specific example in the Bible that highlights this issue is found in the parable of the prodigal son. This time, we're going to focus on the brother. To recap, this parable tells of a father who had two sons. His youngest cashed in on his inheritance and spent it all. The oldest stayed with his father and worked with him. The youngest one came back repentant, and his father forgave him and threw a party for him. Here is how the older son responds, as stated in Luke 15:25–32:

> Now his elder son was in the field; and when he came and approached the house, he heard music and dancing. He called one of the slaves and asked what was going on. He replied, "Your brother has come, and your father has killed the fatted calf, because he has got him back safe and sound." Then he became angry and refused to go in. His father came out and began to plead with him. But he answered his father, "Listen! For all these years I have been working like a slave for you, and I have never disobeyed your command; yet you have never given me even a young goat so that I might celebrate with my friends. But when this son of yours came back, who has devoured your property with prostitutes, you killed the fatted calf for him!" Then the father said to him, "Son,

you are always with me, and all that is mine is yours. But we had to celebrate and rejoice, because this brother of yours was dead and has come to life; he was lost and has been found."

From the get-go you can see the lack of sense of belonging in the oldest son when he says, "I have been working like a slave for you," then goes on to say, "but when this son of yours." Now take a look at his father's response: "Son"—reaffirming his identity and his sense of belonging—"this brother of yours"—reaffirming the fact that when met with genuine repentance, love overlooks misbehavior and reestablishes one to his or her true identity. This is what Christ did for you, for me, and for whosoever believes in him!

Striving through Being Needed

If you find yourself in situations where you feel like you're always the giver in relationships, this section may be for you. This pattern often begins out of desperation. Like I mentioned earlier, you are wired by God to be in relationships with other people. When you experience rejection by the very people who are supposed to accept you, you begin to associate people with pain. Since no one wants to feel hurt and rejected, you protect yourself by keeping people at arm's length. I've even treated people who have gone to the extreme of denying their need for acceptance. They would use phrases like "I only need God." Out of their pain, they bury their need to belong deep down in the hopes that it won't resurface.

Unfortunately, whatever we bury alive will resurrect in other ways. So our need for acceptance doesn't go anywhere. Our brain just figures out other methods to meet it in a way that will ensure we feel the least amount of pain possible. The most commonly used method is to become the person who meets other people's needs. Your brain calculates it like this: if people need me, they won't reject me.

The problem with this method is you end up attracting people who want to depend on you to a capacity that you can't fill, just like we talked about earlier with dependence versus interdependence.

Being needed by people requires a continuous amount of striving to maintain. And although you may feel loved and accepted by the person who needs you, it's only a matter of time before you become resentful of the person who is mooching off of you and upset with yourself for being in that situation. In reality, you were never wired for people to depend on you to the capacity that only God can fill. You're just as loved as those who need you. You're just as valuable, and at the end of the day, your needs matter too!

Striving through People-Pleasing

The closest person to you has the greatest capacity to influence you. Solomon is known as the "wisest person" to ever live. In the beginning of Solomon's rule, he sought the Lord first. In fact, in his early years as a king, God appeared to Solomon in a dream and told Solomon to ask for anything he wanted. Solomon asked for wisdom. God granted it to him. Later on, toward the end of his reign, in 1 Kgs 11:6, the Bible says: "So Solomon did evil in the eyes of the Lord; he did not follow the Lord completely." The Bible doesn't say that Solomon did not follow the Lord. It says he did not follow the Lord "completely."

Solomon's allegiance to God was affected by his circle of influence. Solomon entered into one marriage after another with wives who worshiped idols. It was only a matter of time before he began to do the same. If the wisest man got swayed, how much easier is it for you and I to be swayed if we are not careful.

God requires our undivided allegiance to him. Only he knows it all. Nobody else comes close to how much God loves us. Allegiance to him means that everyone and everything else takes a backseat to God's will. God must be the filter through which you make every decision. Our society is notorious for going to the internet for guidance. God is the author of wisdom. He offers you that wisdom generously. See Jas 1:5.

Not only does God offer you wisdom; only God can complete you. Your spouse can't, your loved ones can't. No one is wired to be able to complete you because only God can. Out of your assurance in your relationship with God, you'll be able to develop a healthy relationship with your loved ones.

As you hold God in his proper place in your heart, when people's opinions attempt to compete with God's truth, you won't be swayed by the majority, because your heart is rooted in God's truth. This is what it means to live out Rom 12:2: "Do not conform to the pattern of this world, but be transformed by the renewing of your mind. Then you will be able to test and approve what God's will is—his good, pleasing and perfect will."

Having an undivided heart toward God is so important that God said it this way in Luke 14:26: "If anyone comes to me and does not hate father and mother, wife and children, brothers and sisters—yes, even their own life—such a person cannot be my disciple." Does this mean that God wants us to hate our loved ones? No. This passage means that our allegiance to his truth must vastly supersede our allegiance to the closest people in our lives, in the small things and in the big things. For example, if you've always wanted to take over your family's business, yet God calls you to another field, your decision will reflect who your allegiance is to. In this case God versus family. If you're interested in marrying someone who is not a believer—although your family and friends advise you not to and you examine God's word, which says, "Do not be yoked together with unbelievers. For what do righteousness and wickedness have in common? Or what fellowship can light have with darkness?" (2 Cor 6:14)—your decision will reflect who is Lord over your life, in this case, God or self. I could go on and on with examples. The point is, only God completes you. God can use people to confirm his word in your heart, but God is your ultimate source.

A word of caution! There will be many instances in life when your friends will affirm your choice to live a life that is contradictory to the life God called you to live. Always remember that the only One qualified to set the standard for good and bad is God. For example, if your friend tells you to go 120 mph on the interstate, assures you that you'll be fine, and you heed your friend's false sense of assurance, guess who will end up paying the consequences for your actions when you get pulled over? You. Your friend didn't have the capacity to set the standard to begin with. The same principle applies to our walk with the Lord. We will have people left and right telling us which way to go. The only One who has the right to set the standard is none other than God. So if you find yourself in this category, where your friends have satisfied your longing for belonging at the expense of compromising God's word, I pray that you will seek God, and I pray that he will remind you of what it means to belong to him and that you will experience the freedom that comes from belonging to God as your heavenly Father.

CHAPTER 11

Healing My Rejection Wounds

Healing from "Works" to Earn Favor with God

You will never heal your sense of inferiority until you understand that you belong to God first and find your sense of belonging in him, as his child.

God wants an intimate relationship with you, not a transactional relationship with you.

Here is the difference between intimate and transactional.

An intimate relationship with God is marked by:	A transactional relationship with God is marked by:
You feel fully accepted by God because of Jesus.	You work hard to earn God's approval and still end up feeling that you fall short.
You're conscious of God's presence during the good times and the bad times.	You don't think much of God until the bad times.
You rely on God's direction in the little and the big decisions.	You don't consult with God unless it's an urgent matter.
You view spending time with God as something you "get to do."	You see spending time with God as something you "have to do."

You know that Christ alone is the standard, and without him, we all fall short of the standard for holiness.	You compare your Christian walk to others', which in turn makes you feel better than your Christian friends or less than your Christian friends.
You consult with God first.	You consult with God as a last resort.
When you make a mistake, you confess it, genuinely repent of it, and receive God's forgiveness.	You're scared of losing God's love when you mess up.
You do things out of love.	You do things out of guilt.
You give yourself permission to say "no" in order to rest.	You overcommit yourself to ministry work and end up feeling overwhelmed.

The point of the above comparison is to draw you to the fact that God wants you for you, not for what you have to offer him. God longs to satisfy your need for belonging in a way that only he can.

In the book of Hosea, God draws our attention to how one can attain a sense of belonging in him: "Therefore I am now going to allure her; I will lead her into the wilderness and speak tenderly to her" (Hos 2:14). Here, you get a peek at God's kindness toward people who have been rejecting him and trying to get their sense of belonging met by other sources. A few verses later, God reveals his heart's desires: "In that day . . . you will call me 'my husband'; you will no longer call me 'my master'" (Hos 2:16).

If you're married, can you think back to the first month after your wedding and the excitement you felt to finally refer to your loved one as "husband" or "wife"? This is the type of relationship God is calling you to. God knows that viewing him as master will likely induce feelings of fear and apprehension rather than closeness. God wants to be both your God and your closest friend. The result of relating to God as your heavenly Father will allow you the freedom to approach him as his child rather than as his slave. There's a huge difference! In Jesus, he calls you his own child, and he draws you to approach him as someone who is fully loved and fully accepted.

God doesn't leave us to fend for ourselves when we decide to believe in him. On the contrary, God knows that his call on our lives can be carried out only through his continual presence and involvement in our day-to-day activities. In John 16:7, Jesus told his disciples that he was going back to the Father. He told them that though they may feel sad about his departure, "very truly I tell you, it is for your good that I am going away. Unless I go away, the Advocate will not come to you; but if I go, I will send him to you." In this passage, you see that Jesus acknowledged his disciples' sad feelings about his departure; however, in their best interest (and ours), he chose to leave so that the Holy Spirit would come to us. The Holy Spirit, also known as the Advocate, the Helper, the Counselor, the Comforter, is God's Holy Spirit. When we surrender our lives to God, he marks us as his own by placing his Holy Spirit inside of us. This is what Eph 1:13–14 says: "And you also were included in Christ when you heard the message of truth, the gospel of your salvation. When you believed, you were marked in him with a seal, the promised Holy Spirit, who is a deposit guaranteeing our inheritance until the redemption of those who are God's possession—to the praise of his glory." When you surrender your life to Jesus, you become God's child. God's Holy Spirit helps you live in the freedom of a son, in the freedom of a daughter. That's what it means to live out Rom 8:15: "For you did not receive the spirit of bondage again to fear, but you received the Spirit of adoption by whom we cry out, 'Abba, Father' (NKJV). As God's child, you no longer carry with you that sense of inferiority that leads you to self-striving. You can rest in the assurance that in Christ, you are fully loved and fully accepted as God's beloved child.

Healing from Being Needed

Jesus said it like this in Matt 11:28–30: "Come to me, all you who are weary and burdened, and I will give you rest. Take my yoke upon you and learn from me, for I am gentle and humble in heart, and you will find rest for your souls. For my yoke is easy and my burden is light." Regardless of how many people have rejected you,

God wants you to know that he wants you. Tying yourself to people who are dependent on you is not the answer. Settling for being needed is a disservice to how valuable you truly are in Christ. God chose you before the foundation of this world to be his child—not because of anything that you have ever done to make him want you, but because he loves you. He calls you his!

This is one of the hardest concepts to grasp, especially if we have gone through our own share of rejection and pain and criticism by the people who are supposed to accept us and care for us. God is not sitting there criticizing your every move. Just the opposite. God is calling you to a greater relationship with him so he can fill you with a sense of acceptance to a capacity that no one else can. Listen to what Jesus says to you in John 15:16–17: "You didn't choose me. I chose you. I appointed you to go and produce lasting fruit, so that the Father will give you whatever you ask for, using my name. This is my command: Love each other" (NLT). So as you see here, knowing that you belong to God as his child is essential to your developing healthy relationships with those he placed in your life. Out of the overflow of his acceptance of you, you will be able to live out 1 Thess 3:12—"May the Lord make your love increase and overflow for each other and for everyone else, just as ours does for you."

Healing from People-Pleasing

My counseling specialty is trauma, so I've often dealt with patients who have undergone betrayals, abuse, and other types of traumas throughout their lifetime. When we experience some sort of relationship trauma that goes unhealed, our brain starts associating "connection" with danger. So when we start to get close to someone, our brain will literally send us "danger alerts" to keep us from feeling the pain that we once felt.

This looks something like the following scenario:

Mary, who has unhealed trauma, meets Bill. Mary and Bill start dating. Throughout the course of their dates Mary starts feeling anxiety or panic attacks. Mary doesn't understand what's happening because Bill seems like a nice guy. Mary starts questioning Bill's motives and lashes out at Bill over little things. Mary comes in for therapy, frustrated with herself for lashing out and with Bill for not understanding her.

If this is where you find yourself, take heart! This is such a typical scenario. And at the risk of being vulnerable, the above not only describes one patient after another that I've treated, the above also describes an episode of my early dating life with my husband. It almost felt like the closer we became, the more I was apt to push him away. I didn't understand this pattern until my training years in counseling. To the outside world you may seem atypical, but in reality, your brain is doing what it's supposed to do: protect you from "perceived" pain. In the case of an unhealed wound, your brain forms a shield around you by pushing people away. You find yourself more comfortable in isolation than around people because at least then, you won't get hurt. While this defense mechanism may serve its purpose in the short term, you are not designed for isolation. Think about it: isolation serves as punishment for criminals; that's why criminals are put in solitary confinement and maximum security. While isolation may give you temporary relief, it also blocks you from meeting the need you were designed to have through healthy relationships.

The question I'm often asked in my line of work is: How do I form healthy relationships?

I walk my patients through the following four-step process:

1. *Heal relational wounds.* In order to do this, you must uncover your unhealed wound. You can do so by seeking therapy or by meeting with someone from the care team at your church. Whichever route you choose, make sure it is someone who will keep the information you share safe and confidential.

2. *Trust that you belong to God.* In order for you to know who you are, you have to get to know the one who made you. As you walk with God, and as you grow in the safety and assurance of your relationship with him, your sense of identity will begin to unfold. Our sense of identity is so important.

God knows this. He gave us this need to draw us back to the source: him. God uses his word and his Holy Spirit to reveal and reassure you of who you are in him: son of God, daughter of God. This is a status that no one can ever take from you! Your friends, your family, your neighbors, not even the devil himself has the power to erase the fact that God calls you his and that you belong to him. Take a look at what Jesus said about this matter: "I give them eternal life, and they shall never perish; no one will snatch them out of my hand. My Father, who has given them to me, is greater than all; no one can snatch them out of my Father's hand" (John 10:28–29). Jesus is clear that no one has the power to take you out of *his* family. Later on, Paul also confirms this in Rom 8:38–39 when he says: "For I am convinced that neither death nor life, neither angels nor demons, neither the present nor the future, nor any powers, neither height nor depth, nor anything else in all creation, will be able to separate us from the love of God that is in Christ Jesus our Lord."

3. *Grow in your relationship with God.* As you walk with God, he deposits truths about you in you. You will begin to see yourself the way God sees you in Jesus. When you truly know who you are in Christ—a loved son, a loved daughter of God—your perspective of yourself will change. You will no longer have the desire to do the things you used to do as a way of gaining people's approval, because you have the assurance of your Father's approval. The desire to prove yourself to people will decrease over time. You will find yourself at peace, seeking direction and purpose from the One who calls you his beloved. As your walk with God grows, you will naturally gravitate toward the purpose he has for your life, which will include developing new relationships with people God chose to be a part of his purpose in your life. In other words, you will be living out Eph 2:10: "God made us. He created us to belong to Christ Jesus. Now we can do good things. Long ago God prepared them for us to do" (NIrV). When you have assurance of God's love for you, you will not seek people

to "complete" you, because you're already whole in Jesus. So out of a healthy relationship with God, you will find yourself gravitating towards people who support his purpose for your life. This means you'll find yourself gravitating toward people who are leading you closer to God, and also ending relationships that are not conducive to your walk with him.

4. *Set realistic expectations.* In referencing our relationships with God's people, Paul instructs us in Eph 4:2–6 to "be completely humble and gentle; be patient, bearing with one another in love. Make every effort to keep the unity of the Spirit through the bond of peace. There is one body and one Spirit, just as you were called to one hope when you were called; one Lord, one faith, one baptism; one God and Father of all, who is over all and through all and in all." In other words, people are messy! We will have disagreements. We will have times when our opinions differ. However, in all of this, we must remember that we are united in Christ. Jesus died for the person who doesn't look like you, doesn't vote like you, and doesn't have the same interests as you. In approaching relationships for the sake of glorifying Jesus, we must be willing to be humble, pray for one another, and forgive one another's mishaps (because mishaps will happen!).

I want to add a suggestion for those who feel that they are "too spent" to spend time with God. Listen! I get it! I wear multiple hats that require me to give and give and give. Between my roles as a wife, a mom, an overseer of our clinical staff, a friend, I could go on and on with reasons as to why I just don't have the time to dedicate to God. However, I have realized that on the days I don't spend time with him, I feel spent beyond measure. God calls each one of us to fulfill certain roles in our lifetime. These roles will change depending on the season we're in. For me, I have found that there is absolutely no way I could fulfill the roles God called me to without him. Out of all of my roles, the foundational role I hold is "child of God." Spending time with our heavenly Father helps reframe our minds to focus on the things that truly matter, and when so many things matter, he steps in and helps us prioritize our life in a way that will give us peace. I've found that during the time I spend with God, I'm able to ask for his direction in the little things and the big things. Psalm 32:8 says: "I will instruct you and teach you in the way you should go; I will counsel you with my loving eye on you." And that's exactly what God does!

He lets me know when I need to say yes and when I need to say no to requests that are pulling at me each and every day. You see, walking through life is like walking through a maze. All you can see from your view inside of the maze is what's in front of you, what's behind, what's to the right, and what's to the left of you. God however, can see the full scope; he sees the maze from above, and as when you spend time with him, he's able to direct you and say, "hey, no, don't commit to this"; or "yes, this is a commitment that I want you to make."

CHAPTER 12

In Christ You Are Accepted

WHEN YOU TRUST IN the fact that God wants you, he loves you, and he chose you, you will find yourself spending time with him and talking with him. The more you depend on him to fill your need for acceptance, the more secure you will be in who you are. Out of that overflow, you will find yourself reflecting the attributes of your heavenly Father that we discussed in chapter 4.

When you trust in the finished work of Jesus Christ and surrender your life to him, God accepts you fully. He doesn't just accept the parts of you that look good, he doesn't just accept you on your good days; God's commitment to you is for eternity. When you give your life to him, he becomes your Father, which means he will love you, he will protect you, he will get in your business to convict you when you don't act right, but he will never leave you or forsake you.

One of the biggest truths you must hold onto in terms of your acceptance is that in Jesus, God has put his seal of approval on you by placing his Holy Spirit on the inside of you, marking you as his. Take a look at this:

> And you also were included in Christ when you heard
> the message of truth, the gospel of your salvation. When

you believed, you were marked in him with a seal, the
promised Holy Spirit, who is a deposit guaranteeing our
inheritance until the redemption of those who are God's
possession—to the praise of his glory. (Eph 1:13–14)

The above passage shows that you belong to God. It shows
that out of the abundance of his love for you, God chose to adopt
you as his own child. Not because of anything you've ever done but
because of his loving nature and the mercy he decided to extend
to you. Belonging to God means that you belong to him on your
good days and on your bad days. You belong to God when you
feel happy and when you feel sad. God's acceptance of you is not
contingent on your efforts. His acceptance of you is a result of the
finished work of Jesus Christ on your behalf. So whenever you feel
tempted to think, "Ugh, I blew it, now God hates me!" or "God can
never look my way after what I've done," remind yourself of the
words of the psalmist: "For as high as the heavens are above the
earth, so great is his love for those who fear him; as far as the east
is from the west, so far has he removed our transgressions from
us. As a father has compassion on his children, so the LORD has
compassion on those who fear him" (Ps 103:11–13).

As you continue to grow in your relationship with God, remember the following truths:

- In Jesus, I am God's child (see Rom 8:15).

- In Jesus, God shows that he is for me (see Rom 8:31).

- In Jesus, nothing will ever separate me from the love of God
  (see Rom 8:38–39).

SECTION 3

Significance

If you remain in me and I in you, you will bear much fruit; apart from me you can do nothing.

—JOHN 15:5B

Chapter 13

My Need for Significance

According to the Macmillan dictionary, significance means to "have meaning." Throughout the following chapters, we are going to explore our human need for significance. You will get a chance to identify how you have attempted to fill your need for significance growing up, how you are currently attempting to meet this need, and in turn, how to fill your need for significance in a way that is sustainable and stable over time. Let's get started.

The origins of your need for significance date back to creation. In Gen 1, we learn that God created every living thing and called his creation good. "Then God said, 'Let us make mankind in our image, in our likeness, so that they may rule over the fish in the sea and the birds in the sky, over the livestock and all the wild animals, and over all the creatures that move along the ground.' So God created mankind in his own image, in the image of God he created them; male and female he created them. God blessed them and said to them, 'Be fruitful and increase in number; fill the earth and subdue it. Rule over the fish in the sea and the birds in the sky and over every living creature that moves on the ground'" (Gen 1:26–28).

Let's break this text down to understand it better.

"Then God said, 'Let Us make man in Our image, after Our likeness, to rule over the fish of the sea and the birds of the air, over the livestock, and over all the earth itself and every creature that crawls upon it'" (Gen 1:26). So, long before you were in your mother's womb, God decided to make you in his image, after his likeness—to do what? To rule over his other creations. So, before you were ever granted any degrees or accomplishments, God made you with an inherent need for importance; and out of your sense of significance, you were going to accomplish tasks that he assigned you.

"So God created mankind in his own image, in the image of God he created them; male and female he created them" (Gen 1:27). The sense of significance extends to both males and females alike. God created both in his image and likeness.

"God blessed them and said to them, 'Be fruitful and increase in number; fill the earth and subdue it. Rule over the fish in the sea and the birds in the sky and over every living creature that moves on the ground'" (Gen 1:28). Long before Adam and Eve ever accomplished anything, their sense of significance was set in stone. They felt significant because they knew they were made in God's image and his likeness; they knew they belonged to God and that they were loved by him.

Significance was a part of who Adam and Eve were as children of God. They didn't have to strive for anything. In fact, after God made them in his image and in his likeness, he blessed them and placed them in a position of authority over his other creations. Take a look: "Then God said, 'I give you every seed-bearing plant on the face of the whole earth and every tree that has fruit with seed in it. They will be yours for food'" (Gen 1:29).

A few verses later, we see how God planted a garden and placed Adam there and that God made all kinds of trees grow. After doing all of the initial work, "the LORD God took the man and put him in the garden of Eden to work it and take care of it" (Gen 2:15). You see, none of the verses we just went over indicate striving on Adam's part to meet the need for significance. He was significant because God made him that way. So what happened to make us have to work ourselves half to death to feel significant? How did we go from there to now making decisions we wouldn't otherwise make to prove ourselves?

Here is what happened: Adam's sense of significance was born out of his connection to God. In Gen 2, God commands Adam to stay away from one tree. God also tells Adam the consequence of not following his command. By Gen 3, we see Adam and Eve breaking the one rule God gave them, resulting in a disconnection in their relationship with God. Out of that feeling of disconnection entered shame and the sense of inadequacy, which are the opposite of the significance held before. Genesis 3 also records humankind's first striving to do away with the sense of shame they felt. Instead of seeking God's forgiveness, Adam and Eve "sewed fig leaves together and made coverings for themselves" (Gen 3:7b). What happened next? God addressed the issue, Adam and Eve blamed everyone but themselves, they lost connection with the One who gave them significance, and ever since then, human beings have attempted to create ways to mend their need for significance, to no avail.

CHAPTER 14

My Striving for Significance

THERE IS NO BOOK in the Bible that better highlights our inherent need for a sense of significance than the book of Ecclesiastes. The words "remembered" and "meaningless" open our eyes to the author's cry for significance.

This book provides one of the greatest examples of someone who builds a life on self-significance. The author of Ecclesiastes reflects on a lifetime spent building on a foundation that is other than God, just to end up feeling void of significance. Take a look at what the writer of Ecclesiastes said:

> I denied myself nothing my eyes desired; I refused my heart no pleasure. My heart took delight in all my labor, and this was the reward for all my toil. Yet when I surveyed all that my hands had done and what I had toiled to achieve, everything was meaningless, chasing after the wind; nothing was gained under the sun (Ecc 2:10–11).

Isn't that how life feels sometimes? A few verses later, he continues:

> For the wise, like the fool, will not be long remembered; the days have already come when both have been forgotten. Like the fool, the wise too must die! So I hated life, because the work that is done under the sun was grievous

> to me. All of it is meaningless, a chasing after the wind. I
> hated all the things I had toiled for under the sun, because
> I must leave them to the one who comes after me. And
> who knows whether that person will be wise or foolish?
> Yet they will have control over all the fruit of my toil into
> which I have poured my effort and skill under the sun.
> This too is meaningless. So my heart began to despair
> over all my toilsome labor under the sun (Ecc 2:16–20)

You don't have to read long into Ecclesiastes to notice how desperate the author feels to find a sense of significance somewhere. He seems frustrated to have searched to fulfill it without much success. As soon as he feels that he has obtained it, the bar gets moved higher and higher; yet he still finds himself feeling as empty as when he first began, except this time he's tired and hopeless. Like the author of Ecclesiastes, we, too, strive to meet our sense of significance using different dead ends. In this chapter, we are going to explore the ways in which we attempted to meet our need for significance during our childhood years, along with how we currently attempt to meet that need.

As infants, we make attempts to get our caregivers' attention. Knowing that we hold someone's attention communicates to us that we matter to that person. The feeling that we matter releases two main chemicals in our body: the first one is *dopamine*, which makes us feel good about ourselves and, in turn, decreases depressive symptoms. The second one is *endorphins*, which calm our nervous system and decrease our anxiety symptoms. In summary, feeling important to someone is an inherent need that results in our mental health well-being.

As children, we make attempts to meet our need for significance by keeping good grades, gaining the status of valedictorian in class, accomplishing things, getting in trouble at school, acting as the class clown, or becoming the one others can depend on, among other ways. As you grow up, your brain filters through patterns of behaviors that will ensure you get the attention you need to meet your need for significance.

Explore: in this exercise, I'd like to invite you to go back through your childhood and write down ways that you attempted to fill your need for significance:

____

____

____

As we get into our teenage years and adulthood, some of our behavioral patterns may or may not change depending on which patterns our brain deems successful to attain and maintain our sense of significance. There are common outlets, which I've also referred to in this book as dead ends, that we tend to use as a means of attaining significance. We're going to go over these outlets and explore the outcomes of each one. Before we jump into the outlets, I'd like to clarify this: the outlets listed below aren't necessarily negative; however, when we begin to rely on the outlets as a means of attaining significance, then we are using them for a purpose other than that which God intended for them.

Striving for Significance: Status

We often fall into this category when we work to achieve our sense of significance by climbing the corporate ladder. While an increase in your income gives you a more comfortable lifestyle, your income should never determine your worth. Equating your title, the credentials behind your name, or even your skills with your worth is a disaster waiting to happen. What happens when the market crashes? Suicide rates showed a significant increase in the 2008 market recession. Even if there isn't a recession to reference, I've talked to so many people who have climbed the corporate ladder, trying to prove to themselves and to those around them that they are worthy, only to get to the top and ask themselves, "Is this all that there is to life?" Listen, there is nothing wrong with pursuing a promotion or a leadership role, as long as your pursuit isn't for the purpose of becoming significant. Take a look at the following two scenarios to help you differentiate between someone whose significance is rooted in Jesus and someone whose significance is rooted in their status.

Scenario 1

You work at a firm, and you have a desire for growth. You know who you are in Jesus. You've prayed for a promotion and trust that if it is God's will, in his timing, it will happen. In the meantime, you go to work. You do as you're told. You submit to your authority as you are told to in Scripture. You have your priorities in order, and you have a good sense of boundaries. So if someone asks you to work late on a night that you have committed to have dinner with your family or a night you have committed to have Bible study, you politely decline and say, "I'm sorry, I can't. I have a prior commitment." After saying this, you're able to rest assured that God is the One who supplies for you. Your co-workers begin to take note of your character. Your boss sees you as a positive influence in your workplace and offers you a promotion.

Scenario 2

You work at a firm, and you have a desire for promotion. You work very hard. You've felt overlooked for promotions in the past, so you work even harder. Since you can't be everywhere at once, you miss your children's games, dinners, etc. Your lack of physical and emotional presence at home causes strife between you and your spouse. So now your spouse feels overlooked and your children begin to feel insignificant to you. The more your spouse complains, which you equate with "nagging," the more you're driven to work later, in the hopes that you can prove to your boss that you are worthy of the promotion. Meanwhile, you have convinced yourself that you're doing all of this to provide for your family—when in reality, what your family wants more than anything is *you*. But you don't believe that, because at the root of this issue is the belief "I'm not good enough, so I need to prove to myself and/or to others that I am."

One Final Point

If you are under the authority of someone who is unfair or someone who is harsh, I want to encourage you that God is not blind to what you're going through. I want to encourage you to seek God through this process, and see if there is anything that he may be teaching you during this period. My husband went through this issue years ago. He had a boss who was trying to find ways to let him go. The bullying was so bad, I encouraged him to quit and that we would figure it out. But he didn't. I remember my husband fervently praying that God would help him deal with his boss. My husband humbled himself. When his boss called him into a meeting and accused him of things that he did not do, my husband respectfully stated his position and continued to work, knowing that God is his ultimate provider. Fast-forward a few years later, my husband got promoted to the highest position in the company and his boss, who once tormented him, was let go. I wanted to share that with you to encourage you to trust that God is not blind to your pain. God is not blind to how other people are treating you. If you keep the faith and continue to display his character, I promise you something good will come out of it, whether it's a promotion or, even better, people will see the goodness of God in you and will eventually come to know the Lord through you.

Striving for Significance: Ministry

Here's how this normally happens: you start a job in a ministry. You're on cloud nine. I mean, why wouldn't you be? You are literally serving the Lord. You begin settling into your role in the ministry, and little by little your responsibilities grow. So one of the first things that goes out the window is your time with God. I mean, God would understand, right? You're spending that time serving his people. Or so you believe! Then as your responsibilities continue to grow, you expect your spouse and your kids to understand. You may even justify your behavior by using one or two Bible verses out of context. Before you know it, your ministry may be growing, but your home life is on fire. And I don't mean on fire for the Lord. I mean in literal flames.

You don't understand why your home life is crumbling down. Your kids may even go astray, and your spouse is at the point of threatening to leave. How did we get here?

Ministry work has the potential of extending our responsibilities beyond our capacity. If we don't have boundaries in place before we accept a ministry position, we risk blurring the line between our call as God's children and our call in ministry. I've come across ministers and children of ministers who have dedicated their whole lives to the ministry, only to lose their more important priority: their family. Or even worse, they get so burned out that they completely lose sight of who they are as children of God, which is our first and most important call. As a result, the ministers are overwhelmed. Their children blame the church for their parents' absence and, in turn, walk away from God, who never called them or their parents to this amount of responsibility to begin with.

Striving for Significance: Your Children

Children are a blessing from the Lord. Our goal in parenting our children is to teach them how to follow the One who made them. Our children aren't here to serve us or our needs. Our children are here to serve him. Some may wonder: Why did God give us children, if not for our benefit? Here is the reality: our children are assigned to us by God to raise them and teach them to serve him, so that one day we will release them to do his will. Our blessing becomes a thorn when we try to use what God has lent us for our benefit instead of turning them over to God for his purpose.

I've treated countless parents who were in the midst of grieving their children's departure from their home. While feeling sad and going through grief is a typical part of life, resenting our children for moving forward with their lives is not healthy. How does this happen? Take a look at the following two scenarios.

Scenario 1

The child is born and is very needy by nature. The parent has been walking with God and has invited God to fill her "significance need" (a process we will go over later). The child is raised to be his own person and is held accountable for his responsibilities. The child grows up and decides to move away. The parent affirms this decision and blesses the child. The child has learned to rely on God first and still calls his parents because he knows that they are available when needed. The parent is sad but understands that this is a natural progression. The parent takes up new hobbies and is able to move forward.

Scenario 2

The child is born and is very needy by nature. The parent has not filled the "significance need" with God. The child moves right in and fills it. The parent's endorphins (chemicals that induce calmness) and dopamine (feel-good chemicals) are released. Everything is great until the child decides that he is his own person and decides to move away. The parent becomes resistant to this idea. The child ends up moving anyway. The parent falls into a depression, unable to accept the child's decision. The parent comes in to see me. At this point, my patient (the parent) meets the criteria for clinical depression, anxiety, and grief. As we explore my patient's history, my patient becomes resistant to treatment, insisting that the child is the problem. As we walk through the natural progression of life as God intended for it, through prayer, treatment, and a renewed understanding of God's nature and his love, my patient is able to invite God to fill the "significance need."

Striving for Significance: Social Media

Just like the other outlets we explored, social media in itself is not a bad thing, especially if you're using it to stay in contact with your loved ones. I truly think that that's how most of us start out. We want to make sure that we don't miss our loved ones' important events, and it's nice to see a niece or nephew's soccer game that you couldn't make in person. Just like with most things in life, if it's not used in moderation, social media could become a means by which we attain significance. The following two scenarios illustrate the difference between someone who uses social media as a means to keep in contact with their loved ones and someone who uses social media as their source for feeling significant.

Scenario 1

You go to an event. You are fully present in the event. You post a few pictures of the event and don't think much of it after that. You look on social media to keep up with your friends and family members and find yourself genuinely feeling happy for them.

Scenario 2

You go to an event. And while you're at the event you're taking pictures for the purpose of posting them on social media. After posting the pictures, you check your phone at least three times every hour to see who liked your post and who commented on it. Every time your picture gets attention, you get a boost of significance. So you get in the habit of relying on "likes" and "comments" for your sense of significance. Now, let's say you post another picture, but this time it doesn't get as much attention. Or even worse, you post a picture and your friend posts a picture, and you see that your friend is getting more "likes" and/or "comments" than you did, so you begin to see yourself as inferior to your friend, thus reducing your sense of self-worth to the attention you're receiving or not receiving.

Striving for Significance: People

People have the greatest capacity to influence one another. In my line of work as a therapist, helping my patients to ascend God's word above the words people spoke over them made the greatest difference in my patients' mental, spiritual, and sometimes even physical well-being, because emotional issues have an effect on physical health.

When we get into the habit of relying on people to acknowledge and affirm our sense of significance, we put those people in shoes they can't fill. And when they don't fill them, we feel resentful and upset and put ourselves at risk of falling into clinical depression.

I'm not saying that we should cease seeking encouragement from others. I've seen however, how relying on others for our sense of significance can result in mental health-related problems. Take a look at the following examples:

Scenario 1

When your loved one becomes your substitute for God.

The patient came in and expressed feeling "lost in life" and loss of a sense of purpose. The patient expressed grief from the recent loss of her parents. On the surface, her symptoms mimicked typical grief symptoms. However, as I worked with the patient, it became apparent that her entire life was built upon seeking significance from her parents. My patient expressed obtaining a medical degree because her parents were proud of her for becoming a doctor. As we explored the events surrounding her decisions, it became clear that even the smallest details of her life surrounded around her parents' approval. The line indicating my patient's sense of self was so blurry that she couldn't tell where she ended and where her parents began. This issue is often found in close-knit families, where the person's sense of belonging is satisfied at the cost of the person's individual identity.

In my patient's case, the loss of her parents shook the foundation upon which she built her life—their approval. Now that the parents were gone, she didn't know who she was. She believed in God and in the lordship of Jesus, but her day-to-day relationship with God was nonexistent because her parents had fulfilled that role for her. In her grief, my patient didn't know how to hear from God, how to rely on God, or how to tune in to God's voice and promptings. In other words, my patient didn't know how to reach out to the One who has the capacity to heal her—that's a lonely place to be in.

Throughout the course of our treatment, my patient learned how to develop a relationship with God. She met with God regularly and got in the habit of asking God for wisdom in the little things and in the big things. My involvement throughout the course of her treatment decreased as my patient learned to rely on God and to take hold of 1 Thess 5:24: "The one who calls you by name is trustworthy and will thoroughly complete his work in you" (TPT).

Scenario 2

When a loved one's opinion conflicts with God's word.

The patient came in for depression and mood swings. As we explored the patient's past, the patient revealed that she and her mom were very close until she got married. The patient expressed that her mom, who is a widow, felt left out of decisions she and her husband made. As a result of this, she felt stuck in the middle between her mom and her husband. As we worked together, my patient expressed guilt about "not honoring" her parent. The patient and I examined Scripture and unfolded what God said about the topic of marriage. We didn't have to dig far. All the way back in Gen 2:24, God made it clear that "that is why a man leaves his father and mother and is united to his wife, and they become one flesh." I would love to tell you that this verse resolved the issue. It didn't resolve it immediately, but it started the process of renewing my patient's mind as we are instructed to do in Rom 12:2: "Do not conform to the pattern of this world, but be transformed by the renewing of your mind. Then you will be able to test and approve what God's will is—his good, pleasing and perfect will." Renewing our minds is a process. It's a process of applying Scripture to what we were taught was the truth by culture, parents, caregivers, etc. The reason this patient was experiencing depressive symptoms was because her life was out of alignment with God's intended will. God is very clear that when a man and a woman are married, they become a new family. As we explored what my patient was taught as a child in terms of honoring her parents, and filtered her beliefs through the lens of God's word, we found that many of the things she was taught were used out of context and for selfish ambition to serve the parents' needs, not to advance God's kingdom. It is through this process of digging through God's word that we were able to "break down every thought and proud thing that puts itself up against the wisdom of God [and] . . . take hold of every thought and make it obey Christ" (2 Cor 10:5 NLV). This resulted in my patient's mended marriage.

Scenario 3

When your source of significance is toxic.

A patient came in already convinced that she had bipolar disorder. As we explored the patient's life, the patient disclosed that she had had to rely on different people for caregiving throughout her life. The patient disclosed that her current source of significance was her older sister. The patient's description of her relationship with her sister matched the ups and downs the patient described in terms of her own mood swings. After further discussion, it became clear that the patient was seeking her sense of significance in someone who didn't even have the capacity to affirm her, much less provide her what only God can provide her. This issue is a revolving door that I've seen my patients walk through over and over again. Unless we learn to find our significance in who we are as God's children, we will be apt to seek it in people who are not themselves secure in their sense of significance; and when those people can't give us what they don't have themselves, we will fall into the cycle of depression and anxiety.

Scenario 4

When your source of significance is good but is not God.

A patient came in for therapy expressing feelings of unfulfillment and abandonment. The patient expressed that she had been raised in a good Christian home and had married a "good man," but that her husband wasn't available as much as she needed him for emotional support. Upon further exploration, it became clear that my patient was expecting her husband to fill shoes that he was not equipped to fill—God's. As we worked through the list of resentments she held against her husband, she was able to see that though her husband reflected some of God's characteristics, he wasn't God, and therefore, he could never give her what only God can. Through therapy, my patient opened her heart to receive her heavenly Father's love toward her and developed a consistent relationship with him.

I could go on and on with scenarios. The point is, if God is not the source of our significance, what we build on will not stand the test of time. In this next chapter, you will be able to practice letting go of the inferiority wound that speaks most to you.

Healing My Inferiority Wounds

INVITING GOD TO HEAL your inferiority wound is so important. It's not enough to stop the negative patterns. The real measure of healing is whether or not God has filled you with a true understanding of who you are in him. Your identity in him becomes the foundation for your positive behaviors.

Just like we discussed earlier in Genesis, our sense of significance started with God. Thousands of years later, it still does.

Getting to know God and allowing him to tell you who you are will renew your mind to the point that it will generate new thinking patterns. Walking with God daily will allow negative thoughts that once produced negative behaviors to be uprooted, and his truths will take root. Once your identity is rooted in who you are in Jesus, you'll begin to behave as a secure child of God.

God gave you the need to feel significant because he loves you as if you were the only person to ever exist. His love for you is great. You are so significant to God that even the hairs on your head are numbered. You are so important to God that he watches over you day and night. It's very important to remember this: your significance didn't begin when you made your first achievement. Your significance started when he made you in his image. It started with him.

Healing the Inferiority Wound: Status

How do you heal the wound of "I'm not good enough"? First, you have to recognize it. Then, come to God with it using "The Steps to Healing Template" (found at the end of the book).

You must also recognize that the temptation to find your worth in your "status" will be everywhere. Even Jesus himself faced this type of temptation in Luke 4:5–8. Take a look: "The devil led him [Jesus] up to a high place and showed him in an instant all the kingdoms of the world. And he said to him, 'I will give you all their authority and splendor; it has been given to me, and I can give it to anyone I want to. If you worship me, it will all be yours.' Jesus answered, 'It is written: "Worship the Lord your God and serve him only."'" In other words, Jesus knew that his status before God superseded whatever Satan was offering him. The same goes for you! Your position in Christ, as a child of God, is much more valuable than any other status you could ever attain.

If you want to live a life that will satisfy the cravings of your heart, I urge you to commit everything that you do to him, which means inviting God to the small and big matters of your life—even the parts of your life that you don't feel carry spiritual significance. The more you spend time talking with God, the more you'll be able to recognize his promptings on your life. The closer you walk with him, the more clearly you'll be able to discern his voice. Think about it: if you closed your eyes, would you still be able to recognize your spouse's voice, or your parent's voice, or your child's voice? You would, without a shadow of a doubt, because you know them. The same concept is true about your relationship with God. In fact, Jesus said, "My sheep listen to my voice; I know them, and they follow me" (John 10:27). So, the closer you draw to God, the more you'll discern his will for your life. Now, this doesn't mean that God is going to reveal his full plan for your life to you in one setting. Walking in a relationship with God and learning to discern his voice is a lifetime journey of continual dependence on him.

A few months after I surrendered my life to Jesus, I felt God's prompting to pursue a career in counseling. Up until this point my education had been specific to the field of business. When God called me to counseling, I was still living with the woman who had invited me to live in her house after I was homeless. I barely had enough money to pay rent, never mind go to grad school. And to be honest, my upbringing was so dysfunctional, of all people I was not qualified to go into the mental health field. My list of excuses was big, but our God is bigger! The more I ignored God's prompting, the stronger I felt it in my gut. So one night, after Bible study, I approached my pastor and asked him to pray for me as I sought clarification from God about going back to school to become a counselor. The pastor asked his group table to surround me, and they prayed; little did I know, the man who would soon become my husband was a part of the prayer table who prayed for me that night.

So, fast-forward a few weeks later, the prompting grew stronger and stronger. So I was convinced that this was God and not just my mind conjuring a thought. One of the reasons I'm sharing this with you is because we will often feel promptings and will ask ourselves, is this coming from me, or is this a direction that God is leading me to? If this is where you find yourself right now or you found yourself in the past, I encourage you to seek counsel from people who walk with God, while you're seeking God yourself in this matter. God's word says if you seek wisdom to ask him and that he will give it to you (see Jas 1:5). And God is faithful to his word. From all I've experienced in my life and as I walked with my patients through some of life's difficult decisions, God has shown himself faithful in directing my steps and my patients' steps. And he will do the same for you if you seek him!

So, I started grad school, and let me tell you, when God's word says he will give you the desires of your heart, he truly does. The deeper I got into grad school, the more passion I felt to help those who were hurting. By this time my husband and I were dating. And by the time I was done with grad school, we were already married, with our first child on the way. Through it all, God provided. As I interned, I continued to seek God for direction where he wanted me to be. God led me to work with children who grew up in dysfunctional homes. To this day, as I write this, it still gives me goosebumps. Because what was once an excuse for me not to get into the field of counseling became a testimony that God used for me to help those kids find hope!

A few years after I was licensed to practice, my husband and I felt led to start a private practice. I was more apprehensive because I was scared of failing. My husband was not. The cool thing about this is my husband did not push me to start the practice. Years after we started it, he disclosed that he had kept seeking God about it. God ultimately put it on my heart, and we decided to move forward.

The practice took off immediately. It grew at a faster rate than was projected for our area. We soon caught attention on the news. I was asked to cover news reports and speak on different mental health-related topics. The success of the practice got to my head. On the outside, nobody knew it. But God did. As soon as I started attributing success to me, phone calls for new appointments ceased. And I mean they stopped completely. For a whole week, during a pandemic that was affecting people's mental health, we received zero phone calls for a new appointment. By the end of this week my husband and I were trying to figure out what in the world was happening. Our phone system was fine. We began to panic because by this time we had several people on payroll that we were responsible for. As I prayed seeking God, I felt convicted about becoming prideful. God reminded me that he was the source of our success; he showed me that I was allowing my status as clinical director to define me. I remember this so vividly, as if it were yesterday. I confessed my sin to God and asked him to forgive me for attributing the success of the practice to me instead of to the true source: him. I went to bed believing that God heard my confession and that he was faithful to forgive me. You wouldn't believe what happened the next day! My husband and I woke up to so many contacts for new appointments! It's like God opened the floodgates. The day after my confession, the practice received sixty to seventy contacts for new patients!

We've never received as many contacts ever since! As I look back, it's so evident that God was reminding me that he is the source of each and every blessing. I'm grateful that when we confess our sins, he is faithful to forgive us and cleanse us. That's the type of Father he is!

God will not sit there and remind us of our mistakes. He forgives us and continues to walk with us, encouraging us to live better. Looking back, I am grateful I went through that. And as I continue to walk with God, in times when I'm tempted to look for my significance in my vocation as a counselor or my status in leadership, I'm reminded of the truth in 1 Cor 1:26–30: "Brothers and sisters, think of what you were when you were called. Not many of you were wise by human standards; not many were influential; not many were of noble birth. But God chose the foolish things of the world to shame the wise; God chose the weak things of the world to shame the strong. God chose the lowly things of this world and the despised things—and the things that are not—to nullify the things that are, so that no one may boast before him. It is because of him that you are in Christ Jesus, who has become for us wisdom from God—that is, our righteousness, holiness and redemption." In other words, our significance isn't something we accomplish by attaining a certain status. Our significance is something that was accomplished on our behalf. We find it when we take hold of our status as children of God. We just need to receive it and hold onto it. When you truly grasp the value of your status as a child of God, you'll be able to live out Col 3:23–24: "Whatever you do, work heartily, as for the Lord and not for men, knowing that from the Lord you will receive the inheritance as your reward. You are serving the Lord Christ" (ESV). When you know your true worth in Christ, you will no longer work as a means to gain approval. You will naturally display positive character traits that Christ placed in you to glorify him, and as a result, you will be able "to live a life worthy of the calling you have received" (Eph 4:1b). You'll be able to journey through life knowing that in Jesus, the greatest status and the greatest calling that can ever be achieved are already yours—child of God.

Healing the Inferiority Wound: Children

This is one of the most heartbreaking therapeutic processes to watch, especially when the parent feels that they put their heart and soul into their children. The children grow up and leave, and the parent feels so heartbroken. This heartbreak can range from "I'm sad that the relationship with my children has changed" to "I resent my child for acting like I'm not a part of his/her family anymore!" Whichever end of the spectrum you fall into, I empathize with you. You feel that you put everything you had into your kids. You may even have sacrificed your own dreams to make sure the kids lived a good life, just for them to grow up and leave. If your life revolved around your children, meaning your children were the center of your life, when they leave, you will find yourself asking, without my kids, who am I?

The pain you feel may run so deep that you may even feel betrayed by them. You may feel abandoned by them. I've even been asked by patients, "Is God punishing me for something?" If that thought isn't dealt with, it soon turns into resentment toward God for "taking away" your kids. Before we look at what Scripture says about this, I want you to know that if you didn't feel anything when your children grew up and left home, then I would be concerned about you as a parent; on the other end of the spectrum, feeling resentment toward your kids for leaving isn't healthy either. Let's take a look at how God intended for this transition to look.

As our children begin their adolescent years, we start what we refer to in the mental health field as the process of emancipation. During the years leading up to our children becoming adults, we provide our children with an increasing amount of independence, while supervising their behavior. We do this with the ultimate goal of increasing their ability to handle responsibility, so that they can go out into the world and be all that God created them to be.

Letting our children go isn't the same as abandoning them. Letting them go means we have raised them in the instruction of the Lord as he told us to in Eph 6:4, and now we are turning them over to God because we know that at the end of the day they are his children. He trusted them to our care, *not* for our purpose but for his purposes that he planned for them before the foundations of this world. So, as much as we care about our children, I can guarantee you that our heavenly Father, who is just as much their heavenly Father as he is ours, loves and cares about them even more.

One of the things that you can do to help yourself through this pain is to complete "The Steps to Healing Template" at the end of this book. This is such an important step, because God will reveal to you if there are areas that you have allowed your children to fill that only God is able to fill. The process may be painful, but I promise you, you'll come out feeling encouraged and freed from any resentment that you may be holding on to.

The confession portion of this one may look something like "Lord, I confess that I feel resentment toward my child for leaving." Make sure the confession is focused on *you* and *your* feelings and not on your child. For example, "Lord, I confess that my kid is a brat" is not a real confession. We confess our hearts to God as a way of humbling ourselves before God and inviting him into our hurts, while trusting that he is able to heal us.

Another thing that I would encourage you to do is commit to praying for them. Now, historically, parents have expressed to me that this step is hard for them, especially since they were upset with their kids. My answer to this is to lovingly remind you of the fact that nothing good can happen from harboring anger toward your kid. Doing so only keeps you stuck feeling tormented. I encourage you to go back through the steps, confess your anger to God, and commit to praying for your child. This does not look like "Lord, I wish my kid would come to his senses and come back home." Praying for your child means you're praying for God's will to happen in your child's life. This looks like "Father, I trust that you are in control of [your child's name]. Please protect [child's name] and draw [him/her] close to you. Please help [child's name] to live within your will. May [he/she] accomplish all that you have created [him/her] to do. In Jesus's name. Amen.

Healing the Inferiority Wound: Ministry

When serving in the ministry, it's so common to blur the lines between our identity as children of God and our service to God.

We start mixing up who we are in Christ with our ministry. This is the number one cause of ministry burnouts. It is why many pastors' kids walk away from God; they see God the way the Israelites saw Pharoah.

If you find yourself burned out in ministry, yet you feel guilty about stepping back. Let me encourage you—the time you spend with God must take precedence to your ministry.

And if you grew up with a parent who was in a ministry, and you felt abandoned by your parent(s), I encourage you to go through "The Steps to Healing Template" found at the end of this book. Go to God with your hurt. He knows you're hurting, and he wants to heal you. Even if you're mad at God because you feel that he took your parent(s) away in the ministry, I encourage you to go to God about it. I promise you he will never turn you away. He will never shame you for expressing your anger to him, because ministry was never supposed to become your parent's identity.

If God has put ministry on your heart as a vocation, please take heed to the following:

1. Your identity in Christ comes from the finished work of Jesus on the cross, not from anything you could ever accomplish.

2. Your ministry should never supersede your responsibility to your spouse and your underaged children.

3. Invite God to every area of your life. He promises: "I will instruct you and teach you in the way you should go; I will counsel you with my loving eye on you" (Ps 32:8).

Healing the Inferiority Wound: Social Media

If you find yourself struggling with this matter, please know that you are not alone. This is literally becoming an epidemic in our society! You have no idea how many people I've treated who were brave enough to come out and say, "Hey, this is an issue in my life." So thank you for being honest with yourself about this! In order to heal from this issue, I'm not going to instruct you to delete your social media platforms. I believe that the best way to heal from something is to go to the root of it, not change your behavior in the hopes that the root will just die, because that method is rarely successful; as we all know, when someone tells us not to do something, it only makes us want to do it more! The best way to approach this is by recognizing the issue at hand, then approaching God with it, using "The Steps to Healing Template" found at the end of this book.

As you practice coming to God with issues, you will find that he is your ultimate Healer. You will find that God will never turn you away. You will find that God loves the authentic you; the "you" that you don't even fully know yourself. And as you continue to practice going to God in prayer, you will discover that God looks at you with love. God, who holds the ultimate authority, is the one who set you apart as his own child. A status that no one can ever take from you. In Matt 24:35, Jesus said, "Heaven and earth will pass away, but my words will never pass away." So, when you feel tempted to hang on to the positive or to the negative comments said about you on social media platforms as a source for your significance, remember, the only One whose comments about you matter is Jesus. He calls you <u>worthy</u>!

Healing the Inferiority Wound: People

Abraham wouldn't have been able to handle his role as "father of many nations" unless his significance was rooted in God's love for him. No amount of adoration from people can satisfy your need for significance.

This means the guidance you received growing up must bow to the guidance of your heavenly Father. This means that we have to examine our lives and, in each of the areas listed below, ask the following question: Are the words my parents/siblings/teachers/friends/co-workers spoke over me competing with the words God is speaking over me?

Here's why it is so important to investigate each area of our lives with a fine-tooth comb: not following the Lord completely led the wisest man who ever lived down a destructive path that ruined his life. What do you think not following the Lord completely will do to you?

My point is never, ever make yourself or someone else the source of your significance. It's a dead end, my friend. You can read about it in Scripture. I've reached this dead end in my life, and I've watched others reach it in theirs.

Centuries after Solomon's reign, Jesus continues to attest to the importance of making sure that God is the *only* source of your significance. In Luke 14:26, Jesus said, "If anyone comes to me and does not hate father and mother, wife and children, brothers and sisters—yes, even their own life—such a person cannot be my disciple."

In this passage, Jesus used absolutes to draw the line between where he must stand in your heart and where everyone else must stand in comparison to him. Therefore, if what your father and mother, wife and children, brothers and sisters, and even your own thoughts disagree with what he says, his word must take precedence.

Does this mean that we aren't to honor our mothers and our fathers? No, this means that we are to place God above them. When you were a child, God assigned your parents the responsibility to nurture you, protect you, guide you, and teach you how to live out the calling God has for your life, so that by the time you reach the age of maturity, you begin to seek God to fulfill the desires he placed in your heart.

A great passage to explain our parents' position in our lives in comparison to God's position in our lives is found in Gal 3:24, which says: "So the law was our guardian until Christ came that we might be justified by faith." Before Jesus, the law was our legal guardian. After Jesus, grace took over as the rightful and legal parent.

All of this goes to say, if you have people in your life who spoke ill to you and you find yourself carrying the hurt, please go to God with it, using "The Steps to Healing Template" found at the end of this book.

CHAPTER 16

Living as a Significant Child of God

YOU WERE BORN WITH a need to feel significant. You will never, ever meet that need in a way that satisfies your heart as long as you reduce yourself to what this world has to offer you. This world has many dead ends that will give you the illusion of significance. Each of the dead ends that we went over lasts for only a period of your life. Only significance that comes from being in a relationship with God can stand the test of time.

God made you in his image, and your purpose is for eternity. That's why none of those outlets work. Your kids can fulfill that role only for a season, your job will fulfill that role only for a period of time, your beauty is fleeting, and social media presence changes day to day. Our God is unchanging, and his call on your life is irrevocable (see Rom 11:29). You are significant because he said so.

When God called Moses to lead the Israelites, he spoke to Moses through a burning bush. While speaking to him, God told Moses to take off his sandals because he was standing on "holy ground." To the naked eye, it looked as if Moses was standing by a bush. However, when God's presence entered the premises, the ground became holy. What do you think happened to you when God's spirit entered you? Right now as you're reading this, if you have surrendered your life to Jesus, God's presence dwells within you. This means you are sacred: holy, set apart as God's child.

So, the question becomes: *How do I live a life that gives me a sense of purpose?* A few chapters ago, we read how desperate the author of Ecclesiastes was to achieve his sense of significance. I love how God doesn't hide the truth of what our ancestors have gone through. In fact, he often highlights their mishaps to show us the hope he offers us in him. It's almost like watching someone mess up many times while growing up. By learning what not to do, you have essentially saved yourself from years of heartache. God uses his word to save you years of heartaches from pursuing one dead end after another. God also wants you to walk in a relationship with him, because only he can give you a life of purpose that will fulfill the desires of your heart. Take a look at John 15:1–8, and let's explore it together to find out how we can live a life that is filled with purpose and meaning:

> I am the true vine, and my Father is the gardener. He cuts off every branch in me that bears no fruit, while every branch that does bear fruit he prunes so that it will be even more fruitful. You are already clean because of the word I have spoken to you. Remain in me, as I also remain in you. No branch can bear fruit by itself; it must remain in the vine. Neither can you bear fruit unless you remain in me.
>
> I am the vine; you are the branches. If you remain in me and I in you, you will bear much fruit; apart from me you can do nothing. If you do not remain in me, you are like a branch that is thrown away and withers; such branches are picked up, thrown into the fire and burned. If you remain in me and my words remain in you, ask whatever you wish, and it will be done for you. This is to my Father's glory, that you bear much fruit, showing yourselves to be my disciples.

Let's break down this passage to find our purpose.

Immediately, Jesus spells out the fact that he is our "purpose-keeper" by stating that he is the true vine. He goes on to state our position: you and I are the branches. He reminds you that "you are already clean." Why? Because of all of the stuff you achieved? No, "because of the word I spoke over you." Therefore, you are clean, because he said so. You're not worthy because of your good works or your achievements. You are worthy because the One who is worthy declared you worthy. This is a significance that no one can ever take away from you.

People often go down the rabbit trail of "well, you don't know what I've done." No, I don't, but Jesus does. If he declares you clean in him, who am I or anyone else to say otherwise? Does this mean you'll never mess up again? No, but I can guarantee you that if you've surrendered your life to him, he will not leave you there; and when you mess up, you will feel that nudge in your spirit to remind you that you are not living according to the purpose that God has for you. That nudge you feel, as we talked about in the earlier chapters, is meant to get you back in line with your purpose. That's how faithful God is.

Let's go back to God's word—verse 4 shows that we cannot accomplish anything of true value apart from God. When I say "true value," I'm referring to accomplishing things that will satisfy our inherent need for *significance*. Something that will be in line with God's desires for your life. Something that the world around you may not understand, or agree with. I'll give you an example— when God called me to the counseling field, I was in sales and marketing. Pursuing a counseling career meant quitting my job, going back to school, and investing in a new career. God wants us to obey his directives. I remember I requested prayer to make sure this was God's desire for my life. During this transition, so many naysayers came out of the woodwork criticizing this transition. Naturally, it looked like I had lost my mind—leaving a field I was comfortable in and stepping into a new one, quitting my job, picking up a ten-dollar per hour job while I was in grad school. When I stepped into the field of counseling, I knew that I was bringing nothing to the table apart from the call of God on my life. Just like with the burning bush reference we had talked about earlier. I surrendered to God, and when God's Holy Spirit came to live in me, he made me holy and equipped me for the job he called me to do.

Section 3: Significance

I knew that my significance came from God's Spirit who is living on the inside of me, carrying out his purposes for my life. God requires obedience. When we obey God, by his Spirit, he brings what he has purposed for our lives into fruition. Years later, looking back, I'm even more convinced now that the patients who surrendered their lives to Jesus in my office did so by God's Spirit. It was all God's doing, and I was a vessel along for the ride who got to enjoy the fruit of God's work. I'm not trying to sound hyper spiritual here. What I'm saying is that our purpose in life, our significance in life, is going to come from laying down our own desires and picking up God's desires for our lives, and that will come from a continual relationship with God. Waking up one day and saying, "Okay, God, what is my purpose," is not going to work. The way it works is:

1. Surrender your life to Jesus.

2. Develop an active relationship with God.

3. Watch how God will begin to lead you toward his plans and purposes for your life, because only he can carry out his purposes through you.

Paul said it best in Gal 2:20: "I have been crucified with Christ and I no longer live, but Christ lives in me. The life I now live in the body, I live by faith in the Son of God, who loved me and gave himself for me." In other words, your significance in life comes from living the life God has planned for you. No other outlet can compete with the joy that comes from living the life God has purposed for you. When you partner with God to live out his purposes for your life, you'll be able to live out John 15:7: "If you remain in me and my words remain in you, ask whatever you wish, and it will be done for you." In other words, being in a constant relationship with our heavenly Father will open our eyes to his desires for our lives. His desires will become our desires; therefore, we will pray according to what God has purposed for us.

In summary: God is the source of your significance. Attempting to find significance outside of God will result only in a cycle of endless striving and heartache. Your significance has been sealed by the One who made you—your heavenly Father.

As we close out this chapter, please know that I have prayed this prayer over you:

> "I keep asking that the God of our Lord Jesus Christ, the glorious Father, may give you the Spirit of wisdom and revelation, so that you may know him better. I pray that the eyes of your heart may be enlightened in order that you may know the hope to which he has called you, the riches of his glorious inheritance in his holy people, and his incomparably great power for us who believe. That power is the same as the mighty strength he exerted when he raised Christ from the dead and seated him at his right hand in the heavenly realms, far above all rule and authority, power and dominion, and every name that is invoked, not only in the present age but also in the one to come. And God placed all things under his feet and appointed him to be head over everything for the church, which is his body, the fullness of him who fills everything in every way" (Eph 1:17–23).

Final Exhortation

Please don't rob yourself of the opportunity to have a daily relationship with the One who loves you most. There will never be anybody who can fill his shoes in your life. There will never, ever be anyone who comes close to loving you the way he does. You will never be satisfied with a life without him or a life that is reduced to an hour on Sunday mornings at church. You were designed to walk with God daily. This is the only way you'll ever feel secure. The only way you will ever satisfy your need for belonging is to belong to the One who redeemed you. Finally, the only way you will ever live out your purpose in a way that will quench your thirst for significance is by living out his plans and his purposes for your life; and the way to do this is by "remaining in Him." He loves you. He is capable of doing the impossible through you. I pray that this book has drawn you to a closer relationship with God, in Jesus's name. Amen.

The Steps to Healing Template

1. Surrender to God.—You are no match for the wound that has been festering in you. But God is greater. Just as Eph 1:21 says, Jesus is far above all rule and authority. He is greater than any wound that has been inflicted on you. Jesus has the capacity to heal you.

2. Be willing to surrender the wound to God.—Approach God confidently in Jesus, and tell him about your wound. In my years of counseling, I can tell you confidently that most wounds are rooted in someone hurting someone, and the hurt person is stuck carrying the pain inflicted upon them by someone else.

3. Ask God to reveal to you the root of this wound.

4. Tell God about the wound. (*This is so important—do not bypass this step.*)

5. Decide to forgive those who hurt you (including yourself).

6. Commit to memory the truth of what God says about you.

7. Remain in God, and trust that God has taken care of the wound.

The Steps to Healing
Template (Example)

Below is an example of healing a wound using this template.

1. Lord Jesus, thank you for dying on the cross for my sins. I submit my life to you, and I acknowledge that you are far above all rule and authority and any wound that I have inflicted on myself or that has been inflicted on me.

2. Faithful Father, thank you that in Christ, I come to you confidently, knowing that you hear me. Lord God, I struggle with wanting to please those around me. I often say "yes", and I feel guilty when I say "no".

3. Father, please reveal to me the root cause of what's keeping me stuck in a *people-pleasing* cycle. Father, please show me who I need to forgive, and what I need to forgive in order to get unstuck. Father, I invite you to every nook and crevice of my life. Search me, God, and know my heart, test me and know my anxious thoughts; point out anything in me that is offensive to you, and lead me to the path of everlasting life (Ps 139:23–24). (Wait for God to reveal.)

4. Father, I remember when I was ten years old, I was in a play that my dad promised he would attend. I remember peeking through the curtains, waiting for Dad to show up to my

school play, and when he didn't, I felt worthless. Why didn't he show up? He never showed up to events that mattered to me, and then my mom, when I told her how I felt, she made up excuses for him. Which made me feel guilty for even being mad at him. I am so mad just thinking about it!

(The point of this exercise is to get you to open up your feelings, your true feelings, to God, and let him get to the root and heal it. God is not afraid of your emotions. Please do not go beyond this step until you tell God about your hurts and feelings. God is faithful. He will show up.)

5. Father, I choose to forgive my dad for not showing up to the events that were important to me. I felt worthless when he didn't show up. I forgive him for the pain he caused me. For the pain he inflicted on me. Father, I choose to forgive my mom for not validating my emotions. I forgive her for shutting me down when I told her how I felt. This made me feel even worse—guilty for even being mad at my dad. I forgive my mom for not being there for me emotionally the way I needed her to be. (Keep going through the list of people that God brings to mind! God is with you, and he is committed to healing you!)

   Father, I choose to forgive [offender's name] for what [offender's name] did to me. (Write down and tell God the story out loud.)

   God honors your decision to forgive offenses. If you don't feel the effects of it right now, don't worry. You will as time goes on. The most important thing is that you killed the root of bitterness, and since the root is what feeds the tree, the tree of bitterness has been cut off from resources and will die as it should. An example of this progression is found in Mark 11:12–14:

> The next day as they were leaving Bethany, Jesus was hungry. Seeing in the distance a fig tree in leaf, he went to find out if it had any fruit. When he reached it, he found nothing but leaves, because it was not the season for figs.

Then he said to the tree, "May no one ever eat fruit from you again." And his disciples heard him say it.

Then you see the result in Mark 11:19–25:

> When evening came, Jesus and his disciples went out of the city. In the morning, as they went along, they saw the fig tree withered from the roots. Peter remembered and said to Jesus, "Rabbi, look! The fig tree you cursed has withered!" "Have faith in God," Jesus answered. "Truly I tell you, if anyone says to this mountain, 'Go, throw yourself into the sea,' and does not doubt in their heart but believes that what they say will happen, it will be done for them. Therefore I tell you, whatever you ask for in prayer, believe that you have received it, and it will be yours. And when you stand praying, if you hold anything against anyone, forgive them, so that your Father in heaven may forgive you your sins."

6. Father, I submit to your take on this situation. Please reveal to me how you see me in Christ. Father, may your truth take root in my heart in Jesus's name. (Wait for God to reveal something to you. Write down what God reveals to you. This can be in the form of Bible verses that are pertinent to your situation; this can be encouragement from God through his Holy Spirit. Whichever way God chooses to respond to you, please be ready to write it down.)

7. Spend time with God daily. Remain in him. Trust him.